Winner of the Victorian Prize for Literature 2024

When Ping leaves Hong Kong to live in the South Island of Aotearoa New Zealand, she discovers that life in the Land of the Long White Cloud is not the prosperous paradise she was led to believe it would be. Every day she works in a rat-infested shop frying fish, and every evening she waits for her wayward husband, armed with a vacuum cleaner to 'suck all the bad thing out'. Her four children are a brood of monolingual aliens. Eldest daughter Cherry struggles with her mother's unhappiness and the responsibility of caring for her younger siblings, especially the rage-prone meat-cleaver-wielding Baby Joseph. *Chinese Fish* is a family saga that spans the 1960s through to the 1980s. Narrated in multiple voices and laced with archival fragments and scholarly interjections, it offers an intimate glimpse into the lives of women and girls in a community that has historically been characterised as both a 'yellow peril' menace and an exotic 'model minority'.

a major poetic work of feminist, so-called 'minority' writing, its originality and brilliance more than earning its space alongside such works as Kathleen Fallon's Working Hot, *Gloria Anzaldúa's* Borderlands, *and Alison Whittaker's* Blakwork.
Marion May Campbell

an unflinchingly honest look at life behind closed doors, where resentment simmers, generations clash, and individual dreams are set aside for the interests of family.
Chris Tse, New Zealand Poet Laureate

GRACE YEE

CHINESE FISH

NEW POEMS

First published 2023
from the Writing and Society Research Centre
at Western Sydney University
by the Giramondo Publishing Company
PO Box 752
Artarmon NSW 1570 Australia
www.giramondopublishing.com

Cover and design by Jenny Grigg
Typesetting by Andrew Davies
in 9/15 pt Tiempos Regular

Printed and bound by Pegasus Media & Logistics
Distributed in Australia by NewSouth Books

A catalogue record for this
book is available from the
National Library of Australia.

ISBN: 978-1-922725-44-8

9 8 7 6 5 4 3

The Giramondo Publishing Company acknowledges the support
of Western Sydney University in the implementation of its book
publishing program.

This project has been assisted by the Commonwealth Government
through the Australia Council, its arts funding and advisory body.

Contents

Happy Valley 1
Paradise 15
Good Luck and Plenty 25
Chinese Fish 51
English Mittens 69
For the Good Husband 89
Sunday Gardening 105

Translations 122
Notes 127
Acknowledgements 135

The Family Chin 陳家成員

Great-Grandfather / 太爺:
1896. They called him slant-eyed celestial oriental mongol yellow peril chow ah fat ah sin ah so alien heathen chinee ching chong chinaman stinky chinky john – he who starched their whites and bleached the shit out of their underwear long after there were no more nuggets to be found in the riverbeds.

Grandfather / 阿爺 / 爺爺:
born in 新寧 Canton in 1903, followed Great-Grandfather / 太爺 to New Zealand in 1921, re-settled in Hong Kong after WWII. Entrepreneur and whisky drinker.
Grandmother / 阿人 / 人人:
born in 新寧 Canton in 1904, survived Spanish flu in 1918, married in 1922, teeth strong as a beaver's.
Mother to four sons and a daughter, all born in 臺山 Canton:

May (only daughter):
daily brewer of 菊花茶, afflicted with bunions, born 1923. Widowed in 1967 when husband Frank (from Australia) died in Triad crossfire in Kowloon.
Offspring: William, Vera, Teresa, born in Sydney. Lucinda, born in Hong Kong.

Robert, Number One Son:
lightweight amateur boxer, calligrapher, trout-fisher, fearsome Chinese-burn giver, born 1929.
Wife Maisie

grew up in 增城 Canton, worked as a waitress in a 冰室
in Mongkok (Hong Kong), looks like Anna May Wong.
Offspring: Arlene, Allan, Archie, born in New Zealand.

Stan, Number Two Son:
avid consumer of Whittaker's peanut slabs, horse racing,
harmonicas, Old Spice aftershave, born 1935.
Wife Ping
grew up in 臺山 Canton, accomplished mahjong cheat,
face like a 叉燒包.
Offspring: Cherry, born in Hong Kong. Lenore, Joseph, Starlit,
born in New Zealand.

Charlie, Number Three Son:
bonsai cultivator, haiku poet, abacus whiz,
blues guitar aficionado, born 1937.
Wife Doreen
grew up south of Oamaru, quarantined on return
from Hong Kong in 1977 on suspicion of tuberculosis,
legs of a greyhound.
Offspring: twins Randolph & Rodney, born in New Zealand.

Jack, Number Four Son:
cricketer, Eagles fan ('Take It Easy'), duck shooter,
devoted to sweet & sour pork with large lumps of pineapple,
born 1939.
Wife Betty
grew up in Kowloon (Hong Kong), collector of '香片茶'
and tiger balm tins, size 8 feet.
Offspring: Tracey, Brenda, Katrina, born in New Zealand.

Happy Valley

In the summer of 1963 meteorologists reported a persistent ridge of high pressure across the South China Sea and there were rumours that the Authorities would restrict the island's water supply to four hours every third day. The temperature was in the Fahrenheit 90s when the 算命先生 on Hollywood Road, who had the entire history of China etched into his face, told Ping that she would marry a wealthy 靚仔, that her firstborn would be a girl and that she would live a life of unimaginable prosperity on the 新金山 at the bottom of the earth.

When the mother runs out of push, they put the stirrups on. She lies with her legs up at right angles, ankles shackled. Don't run away now, the doctor jokes. She's been labouring for thirty-six hours. The doctor stings the mother and slices her open – her flesh gives way like a ripe avocado and her heart beats so loudly she fears the baby will be born deaf. The doctor inserts the salad tongs, scrapes the baby out, hauls it up by the ankles.

The room is silent, the air ceramic. There are no congratulations, no gender revelations – nothing. Until the suction machine starts up and the nurse pokes the tube into the baby's mouth. It cries. They clamp the cord and cut it.

The doors burst open and the Grandmother and the Aunty rush into the room. They run straight for the baby already wrapped in a flannelette sheet. The nurse hands the baby to the Grandmother and says, It's a girl. The Aunty sighs and the Grandmother says, Never mind. The mother – still on her back, feet numb, legs white, nether regions exposed – cranes her head to see.

The Grandmother brings the baby over. The baby's eyes are closed, her lips are purple, and she has a red 'V' on her forehead right between her eyes. The mother frowns. As she reaches out to finger the 'V', the placenta slithers out between her legs and plops into a kidney dish. The doctor hands it to the nurse.

The Grandmother scurries over, lowers her glasses, picks up the placenta and examines each cotyledon: Ah... good, she says, ... 好好.

soon as you born
人人 *and Aunty May*
push the door come
in see my everything
so embarrass! they
wish you was boy
of course but you
ok so everybody
happy I so hungry
past the lunchtime
only got the 粥

The mother-in-law
takes the placenta
and buries it in a feng-shui-ed
location in accord with the lunar
calendar. The hole must be dug deep
to ensure that the child has a long, healthy
and prosperous life.
If the placenta is found and eaten by pigs
the child will lose its mind.

the pig feet soup 豬腳薑醋

(for the mother, after the baby born)

must be have:
2 pig feet
1 or 2 pound the fresh ginger
3 pint sweet vinegar
6 eggs or more if you like (must be boiling hard)

wash the ginger and then dry them then waiting
next day peel and cut the pieces half inch size
fry five minute use the wok no oil then add two
pint sweet vinegar put in the big pot the clay
pot and boiling add the ginger turn the low heat
one hour then turn off then the pig feet pull the
hair out use warm water washing them – the feet
not the hair! then chop small pieces washing
again and put the meat in the boiling water five
minute then boil the egg use 'nother pot heat up
the sweet vinegar and the ginger soup add the pig
feet then put the lid on and boiling low heat at
least two hour waiting for the pig feet become soft
then add the egg – must be peeling first! then
boiling again the egg dark colour add little bit palm
sugar nice and sweet the pig feet and ginger
vinegar soup very good for clean the blood and
warm inside very good for the new mother

Visitors bring the new Chinese mother
a tonic soup believed
to restore her strength
in the post-partum period. It has a very
strong and objectionable vinegar
smell and is made from pigs' trotters and ginger
and all manner of other exotic
things.

There are two weeks in the hospital: silk flowers and fruit, hand-knitted matinée jackets and, delivered by the Aunty, urns of 豬腳薑醋 to build up the mother's strength.

Every evening the baby has her cheeks prodded with her father's stubby cigar fingers and every morning the Grandmother watches her through the nursery window.

On the day they leave the hospital she tells the mother, Ah you are so lucky, your baby has a nice fat face and she never cries, she will be easy to raise.

人人 see your face
she say you must be
good baby no trouble
lucky because you are
girl have to be quiet
gentle you know

The Aunty serves bowls of soup and fuss.

The mother is seldom alone with the baby, not even in the mornings before the sun comes up.

The Grandmother gives instructions at every feed. Hold her like this, she says, not too long now, and when the mother is silent: Don't sulk – you'll spoil the milk.

then I taking you home
we stay 爺爺 the house
and 人人 Aunty May
William Vera Teresa
Lucinda I not allow go
out one month all day
all night 人人 *Aunty May*
watching me say do this
way have to be that way
I don't know what to do

The Chinese mother
rests for an entire month after giving birth.
She must keep warm and lie flat
in bed so that her spine can straighten out.
She must not
wash her hair or bathe,
consume raw fruit or turnips, drink cold

beverages, burn
incense, visit temples,
read or cry.

The 滿月 party is held at The 龍. The baby, a tightly wrapped parcel, is passed from table to table. The Grandmother holds her for the longest time, beaming and flashing her gold teeth at the camera.

There are fifty-seven guests in all. Big round tables with lazy susans laden with so much food they can barely turn, men drinking beer and whisky, women sipping lemonade, the mother sitting demurely in her pink 長衫 and white shoes, eating nothing, sipping 普洱 tea.

As the afternoon wears on her breasts begin to ache and her underarms grow wet beneath the 長衫, which is not one hundred per cent silk as the tailor had promised, but synthetic, man-made, like the children playing under the tables, the babies asleep in their mothers' arms, the wontons in the soup, and the cigar-smoke stratus cloud wafting across the room.

The baby cries all the way home in the car on the mother's shoulder. In the excitement, the Aunty had left the bottles at The 龍. The father, jolly from too many whiskies, chuckles and pokes his stubby fingers at the baby's face. It doesn't help the crying.

Stopped at a red light, the father gropes the mother's thighs, finds a small box.

What's this?

The leftover eggs.

The father pulls out a little pink egg, pushes it in the baby's face. Hey look! An egg! he shouts. When the baby takes no notice, he cracks the egg on the steering wheel, flicks off the shell and eats it.

When they get back to the apartment, the baby is still crying, the front of the mother's cheap 長衫 is soaked with milk, and there is a piece of cochineal-coloured eggshell stuck to the hem.

I so tire my dress my
breast so wet 哎呀 *all*
the men been drinking
smoking 爸爸 *drinking*
the whisky drink too
much then drive
the car you cry cry
Aunty May talk talk
I nowhere to go
headache

They name the baby 小玉 which means Little Jade Precious Pure and Graceful, her father calls her Cherry Blossom.

Late June, the humidity some 90%, he takes a streetcar down to the registry office, leans over the counter blowing cigar smoke at the clerk stroking in black fountain pen:

Mother's Maiden Name: Leung

Father's Occupation: Merchant

Place of Birth: Hong Kong

I choosing
your Chinese
name in the family
all the girl got
to be have same
name 小 mean
small very nice
for the girl

It's August, sticky. The father roams the apartment in boxer shorts and a white singlet stripped hourly and thrown in the bathtub for the mother to wash. *why you talk about 爸爸 in the underwear?* The dogs – great bony wolves – are flopped on the floor, panting on the parquetry. The baby is lolling naked on the dining table, her mother standing close, folding nappies.

Enter the father with his camera. He shouts at the mother: Pick her up! The mother picks up the baby, stands obedient while the father clicks.

Enter the Grandfather, eyes half-closed. 做乜啊?

Aunty in the kitchen makes soothing noises about cold lemonade.

Grandfather sits down in his chair by the window.

阿爺...

做乜啊?

Can I go... see 大家姐 this afternoon?

Grandfather snorts. Go then... go! ... and put some clothes on! He's noticed the mother's brand new pedal-pushers, the ones she bought last week from Wing On 永安.

Aunty appears with a glass of lemonade for the Grandfather, she takes the mother aside. You're a mama now... what about that blue... dress?

The mother goes back to the nappies, the baby gurgles. Grandfather plonks his glass on the table, burps and leaves. The wolves follow.

The mother walks over to the window, the baby on her shoulder. She can hear her husband snoring in the bedroom, she can see the racecourse at the bottom of the hill.

Due to the lack
of marriageable Chinese women
in New Zealand, many young Chinese
men must travel to China or Hong Kong to find
a suitable spouse.
This unfortunately
increases the Chinese
population here, but (truth be
told, the Chow is a lecherous monster, a menace
to the purity of the white races)
the alternative – Chinese men taking
European or Māori women
as partners – is far worse.
1921: 25 Chinese
women per year permitted to enter New Zealand. 1925: no quota
for the entry of Chinese women. 1935: 10 Chinese women
per year permitted entry, restricted
to the wives of Chinese men born in
New Zealand.
1939: Temporary
permits for 256 Chinese refugee wives granted. Conditions:
£200 'maintenance' deposit, £500 bond.
Wife and all children
(including those born in New Zealand) must return to China
after two years. 1948–49: 50 Chinese women per year permitted to
enter. Restricted
to those married to permanent residents for 20+ years
(on the assumption / hope
that the wives would be beyond
child-bearing age).

The father puts on his best tie, the dark-red diagonal-striped one. He's wearing a plaid sports jacket and his hair is slicked back with Brylcreem, he looks dapper in a wannabe-Elvis kind of way.

The mother takes the rollers out of her hair, runs coral lipstick along her lower lip, mashes her lips together. She buttons up the jacket of her pale-blue suit, slips on her slingbacks, clops out to the living room.

Grandmother is holding the baby. Leave her with us, she says, we'll raise her.

Aunty zips up the carry-on bag stuffed full of neatly folded nappies and bottles. Put all the dirty ones here, she says, and here's some 叉燒包 to eat on the plane.

Aunty hugs the baby and the mother tight. Bring her back soon.

Grandmother drops a little red envelope into the mother's handbag. For her first birthday, she says.

Grandfather is sitting in his chair by the window slurping tea.

The mother says, 阿爺, we're going now. And Grandfather says, You going now.

Paradise

For these immigrants
from the impoverished
unsanitary
villages of China,
where beggars and vagabonds are numerous,
and lepers peculiarly wretched,
where the coast is infested
with pirates, children
kidnapped and sold, and whole families
live on boats,
New Zealand is a paradise.

Ōtautahi, the Garden City. Robert is at the airport looking like Stan with less hair and the same stubby baby-cheek-poking fingers.

They pile into the Holden, Stan in the front, Ping at the back, baby Cherry in her arms.

The two brothers talk trout-fishing and old friends, Ping scans the streets for people.

It's night and all that can be seen are the black roll of flatlands, coniferous shadows, rows of squat box bungalows, rooves pitched low.

Their home is sugar-pink brick at the end of a long gravel drive, front door shadowed by an apple tree.

Ping steps out into a million-starred hush – no traffic horns sizzling woks banging cleavers clacking mahjong tiles no hoicking squabbling squawking singing – seven-thirty in the evening, her kitten heels sinking in the dew-soaked lawn, the whole world asleep.

every day I stay
home nowhere
to go just look after
you and Allan Arlene
she go to school every
morning I washing
the clothes Aunty Maisie
cooking the 西餐 *so*
terrible! everything got
the butter and the cream
and the milk and the white
bread all the veggie-table
boiling yellow colour
no taste

Robert has found Stan a job as a welder in the factory he works at, making bicycles. Mornings at seven they head off in the Holden.

Ping is left with the hot milk and Weet-Bix, the baby and the buttered toast.

Flat on her back in the afternoons, the little ones napping, she traces the grooves along the cornices, the cobwebs on the ceiling rose. When the room sighs she reaches over Stan's side of the bed, twists the knob, and the radio makes noises like the meaning of love.

The phone, it rings for Maisie, always *Maisie she gone out, sorry no please.*

At three p.m. she ventures down the long gravel drive in search of the end of the day. Out on the street – there's Maisie, pale and puffy-eyed – *What are you looking at.*

I in the bath
you in the cot
sleep one minute
not even one
minute cry cry 哎呀
唔好哭唔好哭唔好哭
then sudden-ly
bang! the door
shut I scare

Ping dashes across the hall, wet feet darkening the carpet roses, finds the bedroom door shut tight, Cherry screaming in the dark and Maisie hissing, *Can't you keep that baby quiet?*

Two-a.m.-Stan chuckling, She's always – even before – bit strange... Ping seething at his beer-infused cheer.

In the morning a blanket, Cherry on her back. Maisie sniggering, *Village... peasant.*

we never talk about
Aunty Maisie lost
the baby the dead
thing always bad
luck you know

LOVINGLY LAMINATED

Draw-Leaf Tables

An Easy Solution

For Unexpected Guests

Lifetime Guarantee

The cottage is planted in sprawling clover, camellias and concrete pavers to the Hills hoist. For comfort, a wringer-washer and honeysuckle on the wall of the outside toilet.

Ping scrubs the grease off the kitchen walls, the scum in the clawfoot bath.

The first week in their new home they buy (secondhand):

a floral four-seater sofa
a green Formica dining table with chrome legs
a cot for the new baby, born on the last day of winter.

September sees

Stan lighting the fires in the kitchen before leaving for work in the mornings, the back lawn crisped white with frost,

Ping scrubbing nappies in the outside laundry, bringing them in at four p.m. smudged with chimney smoke,

Cherry toddling the garden path in Allan's navy-blue walker, the new baby Lenore (shock of black hair, port-wine flush in the folds of her jaw-neck) sleeping all day in the grimy window-sun,

the next-door neighbours, Doctor M, his wife, their three golden girls: This is a tea towel, a Steelo, a jersey – JER-ZEE, this is how we make Milo, porridge, tea with milk, why you must drape antimacassars over the arms of your one good sofa.

Chinese women
look charming
in their little
native blouses
and trousers. And they have common
sense, dignity, brightness
of outlook and suppleness of mind.

Missus M very
kind lady she
say I learning
fast make
the custard
square

Robert and Stan buy a business frying fish in a little shop across the river: *Bob's Fish Supply,* open six days a week. The Shops and Offices Act (1904) permitted only 'British' shop owners to authorise business trading hours. Their customers are builders and road-workers, burly blokes with spade hands, shovel appetites, 3.5 children and wives too tired to cook Thursdays, Fridays and/or Saturdays.

Ping and Maisie take it in turns at the shop, Cherry/Allan strapped in the highchair out the back with a bottle of sugar water, straws for fun.

Afternoons they find Lenore, a tiny ball in the corner of the cot, empty bottle tossed out on the floor.

we so busy
lucky Lenore
good baby
when we come
home she
still
sleeping

Good Luck and Plenty

The Chinese?
They come from China, came by boat.
Tough lives over there, what with the opium,
the Japanese, Chairman Mao.
Here they stick together
in their laundries
and fruit
shops and restaurants.
They work hard, seem happy
enough. Lucky
to be here.

Stan buys Ping a red-brick house in a sea of gravel and rocks the size of golf balls in a brand-new housing estate. The front door is horizontal panes of frosted glass ribbed like the washboard in the laundry, the bathroom a stainless steel shower base, the living room a glazed hearth, the bedrooms fawn-striped walls embossed with sprigs of wheat, red-faux-velvet curtains for all the world to see. Giddy on the new house smell they skip from room to room on dahlias fitted wall to wall.

> Week 1: Stan flanks the fireplace with two wooden tigers, a silver coal bucket
> Week 2: Ping plants a Granny Smith apple tree in the middle of the yard
> Week 3: Cherry wakes to see a billy goat chewing on it.

why you talk
about the NEW
house? the NEW
house make the
people jealousy
look like we got
too much money
鬼佬鬼婆 *doesn't*
like it you know

The number on their letterbox is 18. *8 is the lucky number fat number mean good luck and plenty.* To the left of them Angie & Stavros, their three little girls. To the right, Rae & Rick, a daughter, two sons, one mother-in-law. Down the back, the Macallisters: two tiny boys, a father (one leg   ) *Whadda YOU looking at.* The billy goat belongs to Angie & Stavros.

Please.
If we must have immigrants
let them come from Britain.
I have no ill feeling whatsoever against
the colour of a man's skin,
but we must face facts. Most
New Zealanders do not
want foreigners.
Look at what the large importation of aliens
has done to Australia. Ask
any *real* Australian what
he thinks of the New Arrivals. Let's fill our
lovely country with our *own*
kind.
Yours, etc. A STERLING KIWI.

In the classroom neighbour Rae does all the talking. This is Cherry, doesn't speak much English (一句唔識講) ... that's right, she'll learn, bright little thing. Her mother's hunched over a tiny table, leaving a parting gift: a skinny green crayon house with a high-pitched roof, fat curtains, no door or chimney to let out the heat – 媽媽? 媽媽!

Missus L's legs pooling at the ankles, blue-eyed dolls on the wall not-blinking, a smiling sun, fat-cheeked wind, black-eyed rain, bells ringing, pink-faced boys chanting nah-na-na-nah-na-nah-na-na-nah-na... *What's the weather today boys and girls?*

Frequently, Chinese
children know not
one word of English
when they begin school. The transition would be
so much easier if their parents made
the effort to expose them to our language from
infancy. It is difficult,
however, because the majority of them insist on sticking
to their own kind.

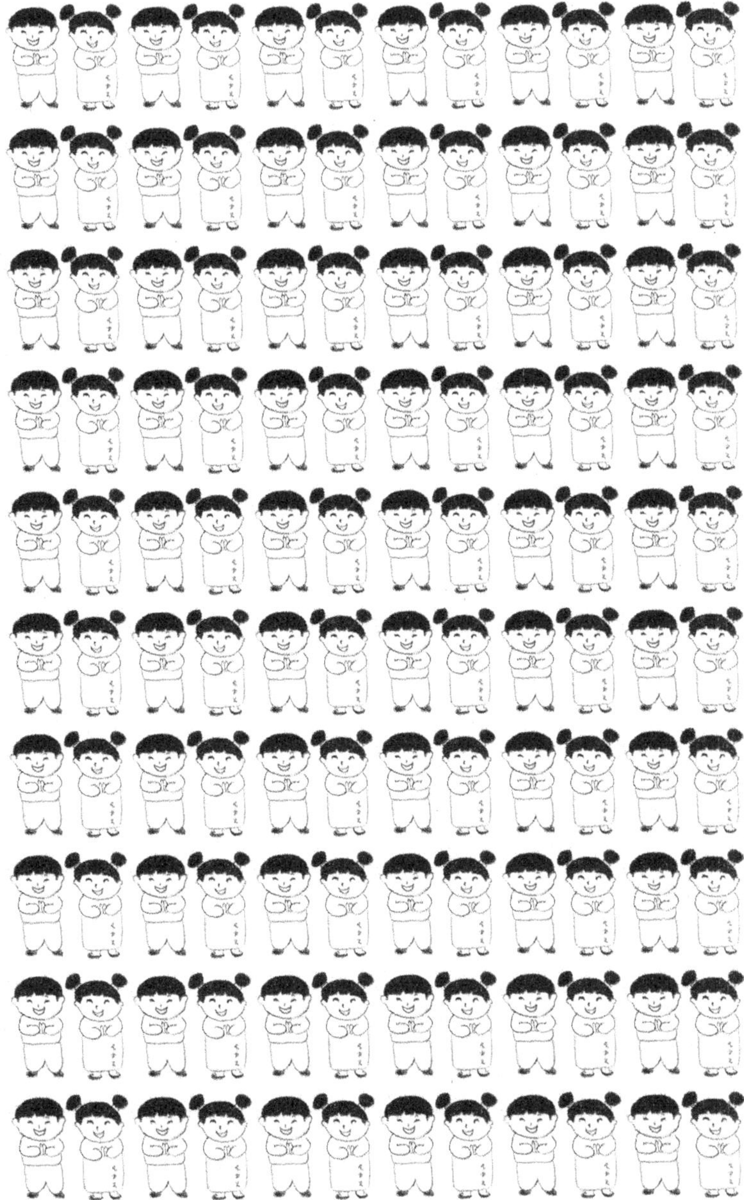

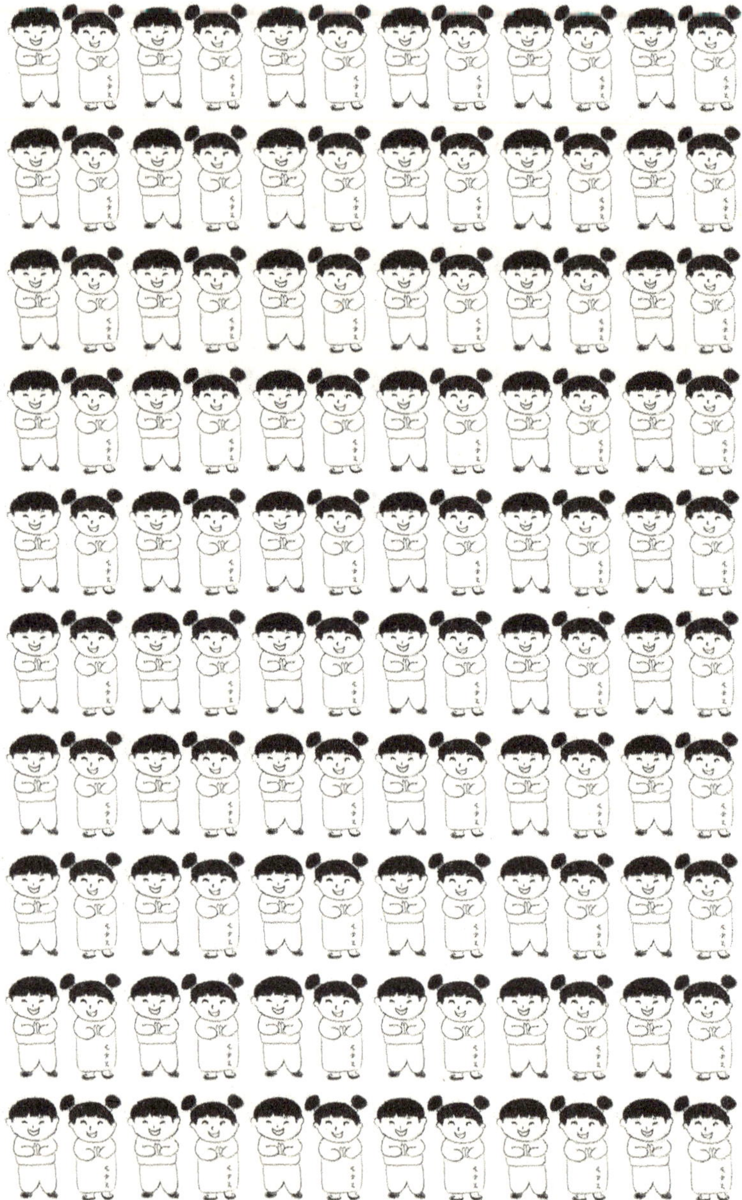

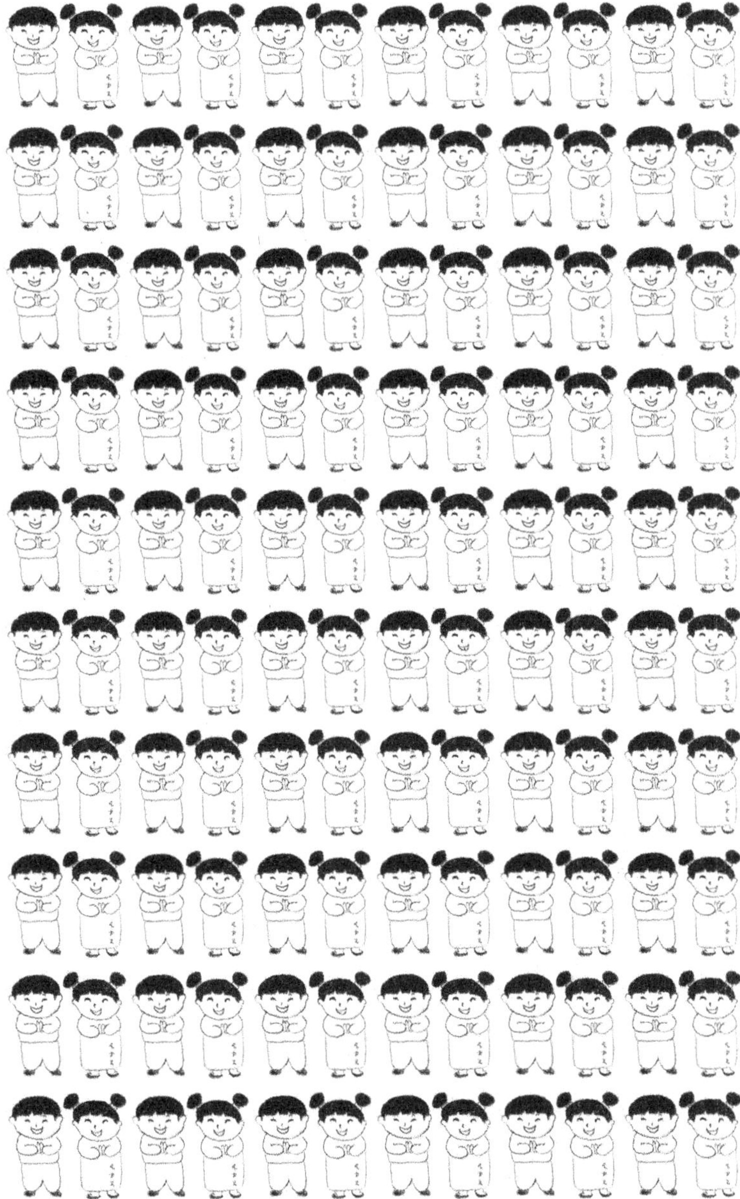

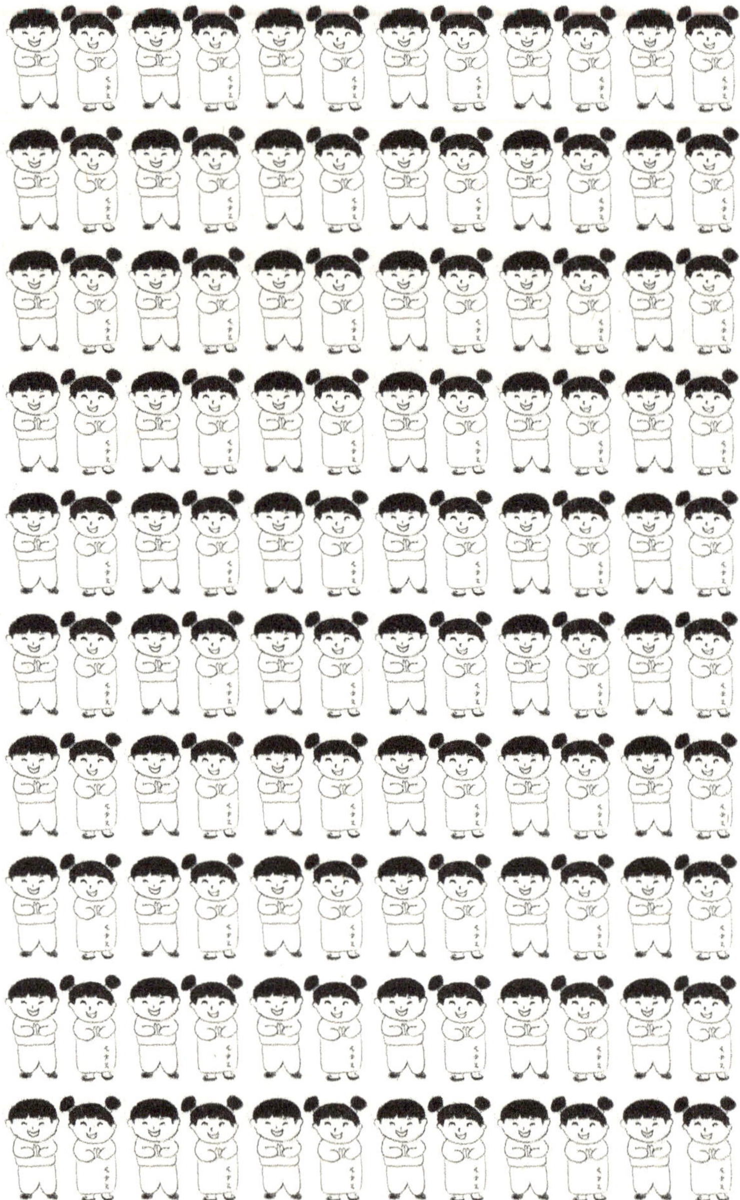

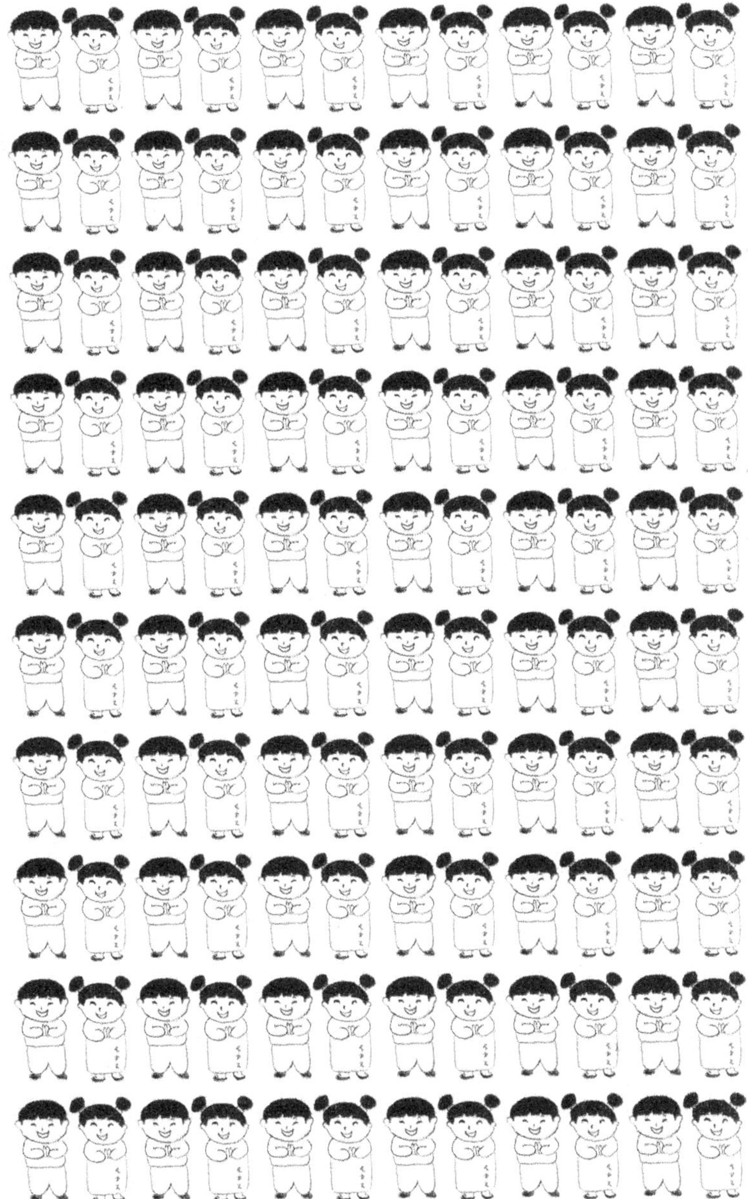

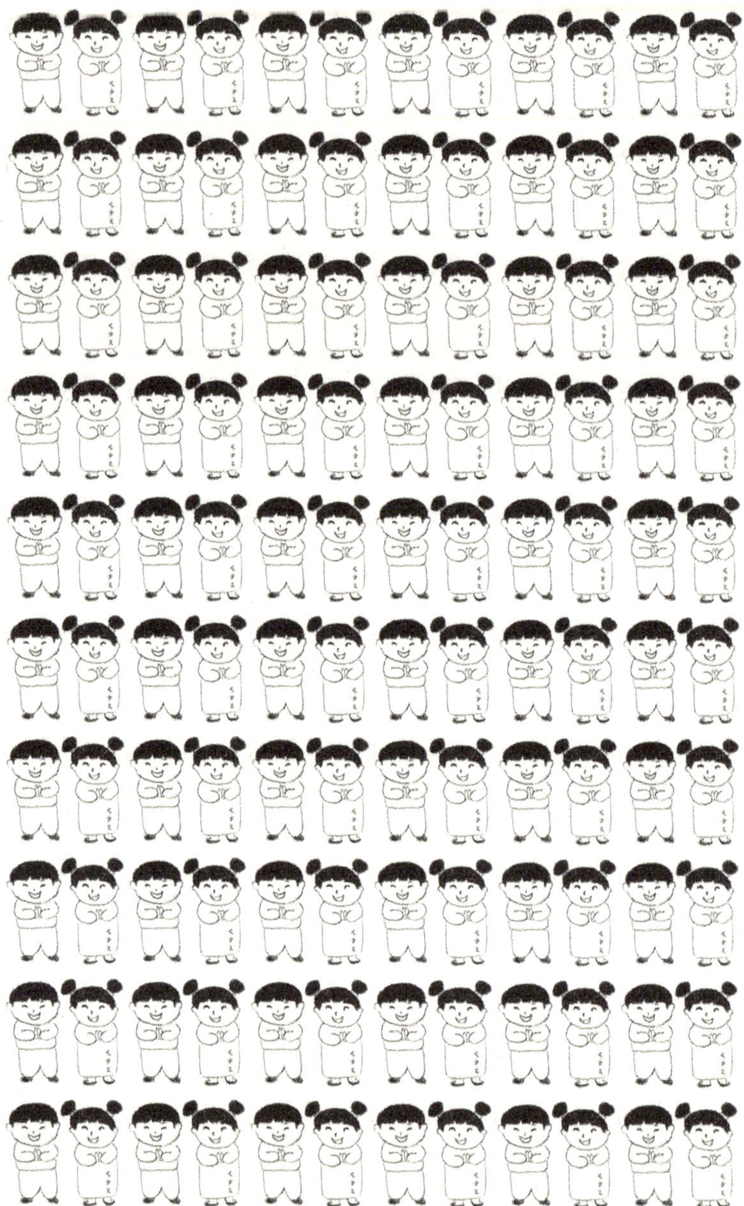

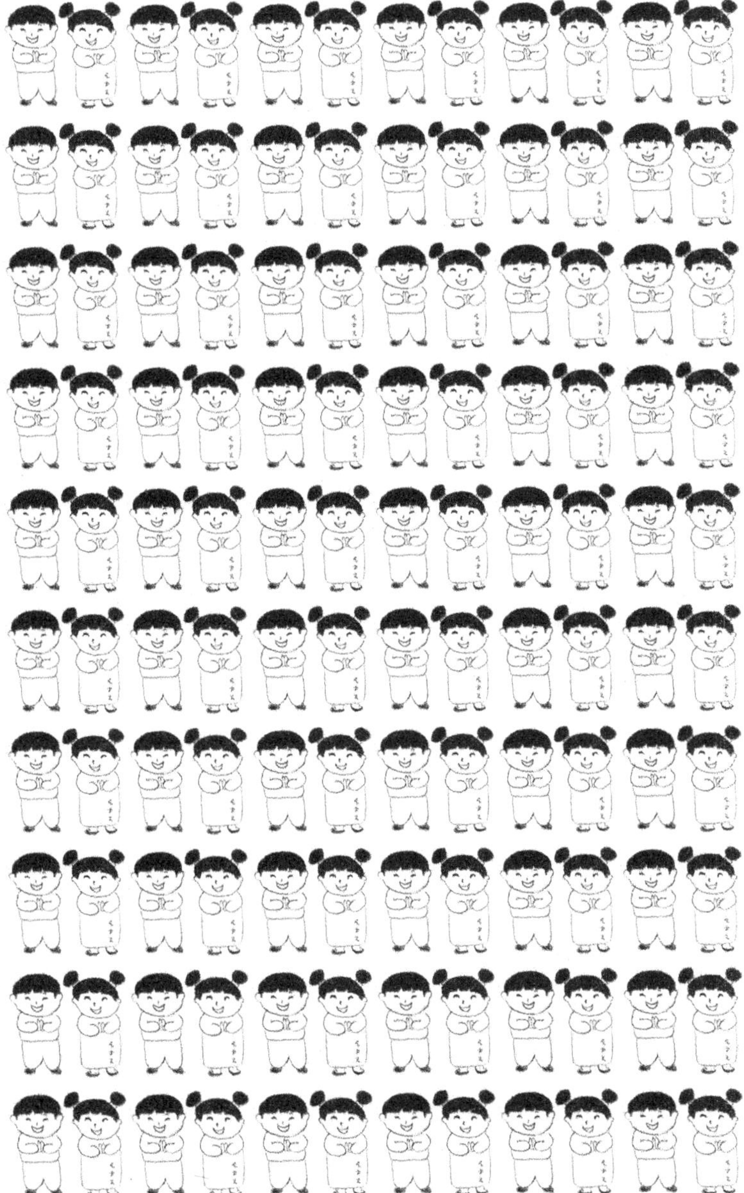

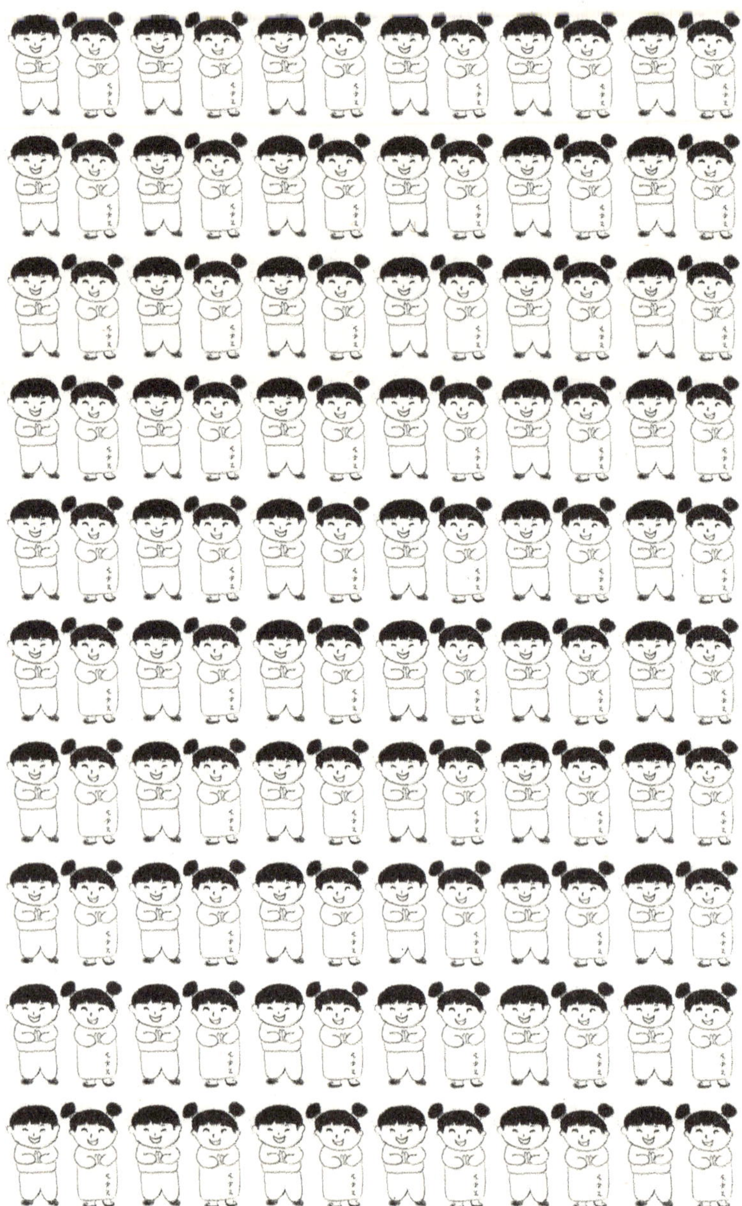

Tuesday afternoon. Chrome silver teapot on a raffia mat and pink iced finger buns straight out of the oven, sticky, cut and smeared with butter. Baby Joseph in the highchair kicking, bottle of milk in a saucepan on the stove. Tap at the back door and Angie waddles in, baby on her bladder (sucks all the air out of the kitchen).

You heard Rae's new puppy? barks all bloody night how's anyone supposed to get any sleep keep the damn dog inside at night how hard is that bloody dog got this one kicking and Shelley's blimmin' teeth Stavros snoring no chance of getting any sleep I told Rae I told her keep the bloody dog inside know what she said but then he keeps us awake so considerate ay just keep the whole street up why don't you long as you get your beauty sleep darlin' don't give a shit about anyone else...

Ping nodding smiling pouring tea.

MIGHTY SAVING!

MIGHTY TEA

29C *HALF POUND*

JUST ONE

OF THIS WEEK'S

SUPER SPECIALS!

I drinking
tea with
milk now
getting
used
to it

In the eyes of the mainstream Cherry's peeling the banana leaves off the 糭 in her lunchbox, fist hidden under the lid, when the seagulls land – Yougotfriedrice?chowmein? wheresyachopsticks?wewannaseewewannaseewewanna see whats*that*? Steamed rice... Whatsthat*pinkthing*? Lup cheong 臘腸... Lupwhat?!gizalook!ewww!yuck!urrrgh!ewwwwwwww.....! They all fly away and the sky too-blue too-ewwwwwww! stings her eyes but Delia's still there, hovering over her shoulder, face like a goldfish blinking they were strange and Other.

they want
sandwichee
for lunch
sandwichee
how can
feel full?
how?

哎呀! What's the matter with Cherry? Skinny like a chopstick! Betty shooshes Robert, plants a chicken wing in Cherry's bowl of rice. Eat more, ah?

It's Saturday night at AuntyBettyUncleJack's and everybody's there except Stan, crowded around the rosewood table in the tiny dining room with the blue floral carpet and AuntyBettyUncleJack in their wedding finery looking down from the picture rail.

Platters of 冬菇 slick with oyster sauce, snow peas and cashews – These the snow peas you grew? – crispy-skinned flounder, whitebait patties – Too much salt! – tureens of lotus root soup – Many lotus roots left? Nearly all gone, you? 阿爺 will bring some – glass bottles of Fanta Coca-Cola Leeds – Who drank all the lemonade? More rice?

At 11.45 p.m. the mahjong game is still going strong. The babies, worn out from sliding down the banisters, lie curled up on the floor beneath their mothers' feet.

Allan and Cherry sit cross-legged in front of the grandfather clock in the hall, willing its brassy hands and singing *to see what we could see see see...* When the gong strikes midnight they fling open the living room door –

It's twelve o'clock, time to go home!

The mothers sigh-stretch and demolish the wall, they gather up their winnings and their babies.

Turning into the garage, Ping's headlights burn where Stan's car should be. Shaking the children awake, she hustles them to the front door, fumbles with the keys, and the house is refrigerator-cold. They stagger to their rooms and fold fully dressed into goose-down quilts (haw flakes rotting our molars as we sleep).

Stan returns at three a.m., falls into bed reeking of beer and cigarettes, reaches under Ping's nightgown, her elbow in his gut, his vomit all over the pink candlewick.

every night he
go out come
home two three
clock I can't sleep
I waiting for him
use the vacuum
cleaner try to SUCK
all the bad thing out

Angie's living room. The little ones sprawled on the floor watching Bewitched on TV, Ping perched on the sofa piled high with sheets and towels and souvenirs from Australia. We had *such* a good time didn't we kids? How do you like this Ping? Angie (nose twitching like samantha's) clutching a curly-haired doll with blue eyes that open-shut, skirt made of shells. Found her at the market, jeez they had good stuff there, look at these! Tea towels printed with maps of Australia, boomerangs and kangaroos, dotted circles on their flanks. Which ones do you want? Ping smiles, shakes her head. Up until December 1972, Chinese New Zealanders were only eligible for 72-hour visas when visiting Australia. Other New Zealanders were granted 3-month visas. These'll look good in your kitchen – and here's some wee koalas for the kids. This – *this* – is the best! Look. You screw it in the wall, put your loo paper here... tunes into all the stations. Angie turns the dial and Neil Diamond is singing... (so everybody wants one)

Summertime. Rice, stir-fried cabbage and pork, dinner in the kitchen is easy, the back door open, lambs frying over the fence.

I didn't kill the fuckin' dog, Jesus Stavros, whaddya take me for?

You said you –

Nothin', I said nothin' –

You said you were gonna –

I said I *wanted* to...

Like a thousand times.

It wasn't me.

Then who Angie, who?

How the hell would I know? Kids...

Who?

That Rae bitch – how dare she fuckin' blame me –

She didn't.

You heard her – *did you give Jojo anything to eat this morning*?

She was just asking –

She was accusing.

But you're happy now aren't you?

Whadda *you* think?

I dunno what to think.

Jesus Christ, maybe we can all get some sleep now.

Rae doesn't like
Angie
Angie doesn't like
dog
dog doesn't like
meat
so dead at least
now no more
noise

CHOP CHOP!

BBQ Lamb cutlets & tomato sauce

Curried chops

Soy sauce chops

Mint sauce chops

Sweet & sour chops

Hot-pot chops

Casserole of chops & apple

Casserole of chops & vegetables

Chops, chips & peas

Lunch is roast chicken potatoes pumpkin carrots boiled peas sachet-gravy apple pie and a vanilla sponge birthday cake baked in a casserole pot, white blackout candle planted in the middle. They all crowd around the kitchen table singing Happy Birthday to Baby Joseph standing on a stool in his green checkered shirt and best corduroy pants.

(because joey + knives = *WILD THING*) Ping makes the first cut into the sponge with a bread knife and Cherry cuts the cake into squares, serves it straight into everyone's hands. There are only six chairs around the table, so most of them eat standing up. Aunty Betty says, Hmmm good – how many eggs?

The father-uncle-brothers sit on the front step smoking cigarettes, watching over their babies sucking rocks in the drive,

Charlie strumming the guitar, Stan blowing the harmonica. The girls are in the bedroom, hairbrush popstars so vain (we really think the songs are about us), the mothers washing up in the kitchen.

They'll be here soon. Who? 阿爺? Veeery soon. Got your room sorted? What! We had them last time. We haven't fixed that broken window yet. Only one room at our place. Maisie Betty Doreen laughing, No choice Ping.

when 爺爺 stay
our house we cooking
cleaning making the tea
never complain 爺爺 is
the boss whole family
Maisie Betty Doreen
and me we all good
daughter-in-law
whatever he want
we say 'ok' that's why
they choosing us

It's twenty-four degrees, the plane has landed, and the little ones, faces pressed against the windows, are watching the baggage handlers and their carts, the stairs-on-wheels across the tarmac, the air hostess smiling, her lips moving. There's Grandfather, lean and darkly suited, gripping the handrail, and Grandmother stout in blue brocade.

Quick quick! Aunty Maisie's lining up the little ones from tallest and eldest to youngest and smallest, Baby Joseph wide-eyed in brown corduroy at the end of the line.

Here's Grandfather shaking hands with Robert Stan Jack and Charlie, grunting at their wives, and Grandmother, handbag over her arm like Queen Elizabeth, squeezing Baby Joseph's fat apple cheeks 你咁乖仔嘅! Grandfather handing out twenty-dollar bills, the little ones mumbling, 多謝爺爺多謝 (all of our eyes on the ground).

The Chinese woman
has a slender figure and a miserable life, yet she
neither diets nor exercises. She enjoys few
of the freedoms or happiness
of our own women, and her
proportions are ideal
for the slim-fitting tunics that will never
be entirely discarded for Western
dress.

you was seven
man knock the door
looking for 爸爸 he
want money lots
of money man said
better pay quick
The full extent
of her subjection
is only realised
when she strives
I said what's
problem? why?
most wholeheartedly
in her endeavours
to meet the obligations
prescribed for her
he
has
'nother
daughter
'nother woman!
how
I put up? how
I put up? but
I put up

Sunday afternoon, Betty & Jack's house:

Betty Doreen Arlene & Tracey in the kitchen mashing bananas for cake

Baby Joseph & Baby Katrina in the front bedroom sleeping

Maisie & Baby Archie in the outside toilet crouching sitting

Allan & Cherry in the dining room bickering over the Monopoly board

Robert Stan Jack & Charlie in the living room smoking behind the sports pages (headline: Muhammad Ali Broken Jaw)

Randolph & Rodney under the stairs cornering the cat

Brenda & Lenore in the backyard swinging from the plane tree

Grandfather doing laps around the sprawling front lawn

Grandmother on the verandah step shelling peas

Ping in the glasshouse, picking weeds and weeping

Chinese Fish

Chinese food
is supposed to be good, but it is strange and uncanny.
In a bowl of clean water there were several
things that looked like the specimens
that are kept in spirits in surgeons' museums. 'Fish!'
explained the cook. 'What sort?' 'Oh,
Chinese fish!'

in summer my mother stomped around the house
in bare feet. she didn't pad, she stomped.
she stomped because she hated the heat, the house
and raising children in the heat in the house.
she stomped because god had given her a gambling man
and a job frying fish six days a week.

at night when all was done for the day, my mother
would sit on our second-hand hemp sofa, tuck her feet
sideways like a mermaid and watch television. she liked
selwyn toogood's 'money or the bag' because she wanted
to win the sewing machine, and she loved
the annual miss universe pageant because she wanted to win
that too. she would ask my ogling father if he thought she
was as pretty as miss hong kong.

I would be sprawled on the floor with a book
not far below her feet. my mother's feet
were the colour of cooked chicken (though bonier)
and the heels were cracked dry and black. she never
had the urge to moisturise or to do that thing
where you slough off the dead skin: *exfoliate.*

I yearned to pull at the crusty bits myself,
sure that if I could yank the skin off I would find my real
mother underneath. but we were forbidden to touch
any part of her body. (joey stroked a toe one day,
and for his trouble received a kick and a blood nose)

when my mother dressed up to go out
she would spend hours setting her hair
and powdering her face and she'd put her feet
in pretty sandals. that her crusty black heels
were on show didn't seem to bother her in the slightest.

I think they were her parting shot, a way of saying
as she left a place: yes, I do look nice, don't I?
but *look how hard I have to work for it.*

must be wrap
the money in
the newspaper use
the old basket go
to bank no one can
see I wear the dirty
smock scarf my hair
look like the poor
but Because there
prevailed a belief that
'chinamen' took what
Pākehā believed was
rightfully 'theirs' ***we***
always washing the
feet before sleep

The rules laid down for the management of children are very few. They are to be kept clean, they are not to be allowed to eat and drink gluttonously, nor to play too much for fear of contracting idle habits.

After school they watch Johnny the Potato Boy load up the chipmaker. Evenings when the shopfront is full of customers they're out on the street sucking sweet cigarettes, blowing haloes (just like 爸爸) on the windows of the TAB. Dinner is plain rice and steamed fish & ginger on the rickety fold-out table, the spud-washer clunking-whining. Best part of the day: watching Stan sweep water across the cement floor into the drain with the big squeegee mop. (that and checking the rat-traps for prey)

shop VERY clean EVERY
day mop the floor catch
the rat 死鬼佬 *why they*
tip all the chip out touch
the fish 哎呀 *what they*
looking for? Under the
Opium Prohibition Act (1901)
and the Dangerous Drugs Act
(1927), New Zealand police
had powers to conduct
random searches on Chinese
businesses and residences
without warrant (until 1965).
they never asking me
just make big mess
死鬼佬最憎...

'Just going to have a look round,' says the Inspector. 'All li',' replies the shopkeeper, and a door at the back of the shop admits us to the kitchen. Five Chinese are eating rice and curry, using their chopsticks with wonderful dexterity. The eating utensils are very clean, but the kitchen is littered with all kinds of rubbish and the floor is appallingly dirty. A Chinaman glides along a pace or two behind during the inspection. 'Look here, you must clear this rubbish out,' says the Inspector. 'All li'. Clear 'im out. Thank you.' Over it all broods the sour smell of Asia.

The health-inspector-man is marching around the back of the shop in his slick black shoes, poking and prodding his hairy sausage fingers through buckets of chip-cut potatoes, trays of filleted fish and bags of flour, Ping *yes sir, of course fresh!* picking up tidying straightening in his wake, all the while boring an evil eye through the back of the health-inspector-man's sweaty red neck.

What's this? the health-inspector-man shouts, big nose in a barrel by the back door.

Fat, says Stan.

What's it for?

Make soap.

Soup?

Soap!

And these?

Oyster shell.

When the health-inspector-man leaves, Baby Joseph dips his pink-and-peeling-eczema-fingers in the oyster shell bin. No! Stan nudges Baby Joseph aside, kicks the bin under the counter. Baby Joseph sits down on the wet cement floor, kicks and screams. (lenore and I roll eyes over our mound of floury sausages)

When Ping, wound white and tight as a snake, charges at Baby Joseph, clog in hand, Stan scoops him up, marches out the back door past the TAB the greengrocer the butcher's shop to the old wooden shed, where he plants him in a pile of cardboard boxes, bolts the door.

The butcher – in blood-spattered navy-&-white-striped apron and gumboots – appears at the front of the shop holding Baby Joseph by the hand. Baby Joseph is holding a cone with two scoops of rainbow-coloured ice-cream. He's sniffing and licking.

Ping and Stan make sounds like laughter.

The butcher winks at Cherry and Lenore peeking between the fly-strips. You girls want ice-cream?

They nod and skip out the door but not before Stan presses a dollar bill into Cherry's hand. Get me a packet of Rothmans.

FRACAS IN A LAUNDRY. EUROPEAN V. CHINESE.
Ernest Ferguson, a boilermaker, said he went to the laundry
managed by Wing Lee
on Saturday 23rd April to get his clothes. Mr
Herdman: is it not a fact that you were in a fightable
frame of mind, that you had been drinking
and felt like fighting
all the Chinese in the country? Witness said that
Ferguson was defending himself, with his hands by his side,
and waiting for the Chinaman
to hit him, 'as any man would do'. Counsel submitted
that it was a piece of gross and unwarranted impertinence
on Ferguson's part to have gone behind
the counter. Wing Lee was a decent law-abiding and peaceful
citizen, who had carried on his business in a perfectly
reputable manner.

Friday night, the shopfront is packed with builders from the construction site across the river. The vats are bubbling, Ping is shuffling baskets, Stan's salting wrapping whistling shouting – three fish! three sau-sa-jaaaah! three chip! – drumming the countertop with stubby cigar fingers. It's all going swimmingly until the phone rings and Stan ducks out the back.

Returning with an armload of paper, he spies a ginger-haired hand on the till – hey! – drops the paper on the counter with a thud.

Ginger looks up, blue eyes startled.

You try to take my money? Stan opens the till, scans the drawer, slams it shut.

Nah... Ginger steps back, hands in his pockets.

I saw you!

Nah... Ginger says, I had me hand... here, and he places a palm gingerly on the countertop.

I saw your hand *on the till.*

Nah –

You better go!

But –

I'll call the police!

I done nothin' –

You better go now!

What about me chips?

Stan steps out from behind the counter, Ginger scans the other customers, they all avert their eyes.

You better go! Stan's at the door holding the fly strips aside.

For ten long seconds there's nothing but the splutter of wet battered fish burning in the vats, Ping watching her husband her heart *I scare* going boom-boom-boom.

When Ginger steps out muttering, Stan turns to the other customers eyes wide and shouts, I saw him! They all shuffle their feet and clear their throats. Yeah he looked like trouble, I saw him too, sneaky bugger.

tonight god is me:
        clopping in my mother's white beaded shoes
                and grey chinchilla coat
the babysitter has left the dishes to sink her boyfriend
        in the sofa
                I swing my father's shotgun, curl the trigger
                        shoot my sister upside down
                                in the mirror laughing
                we spray the air with mama's best perfume
                        the mist settles on the lids of our new
                                blue eyes, we don't even blink
        when baby brother cries we feed him bullets on the bed

When Ping discovers she is pregnant with her fourth child, the first thing she says is, 哎呀 哎呀 哎呀 四四四… 死死死…

The Chinese
are very superstitious.
The number four
is considered to be supremely unlucky.
They will go to much trouble to avoid houses,
telephone numbers, floors, and car registration plates
with the number four. Their unease is so firmly wrought
(and so absurd) that some families
blessed with four
children, feel it a matter of urgency to go on
to have five.

It's five p.m. and Missus A (snow-white hair, silver-rimmed glasses, two-fish-and-two-scoops-of-chips-please) is whispering urgently over the counter. *All mothers need eyes at the back of their head.*

Ping (longing for eyes to see past her belly): OK.

You're so busy dear, why don't you let me look after them?

You sure no trouble?

So beginning a new Friday night routine: three children for two hours in exchange for one pound of groper.

Missus A lives in a tiny two-bedroom flat with her 36-year-old unmarried son Raymond. Call me Clarice, she sings, it rhymes with Paris!

At the park with the paddling pool, buk choy dregs floating in the murk, she shouts, Here we go, take off your clothes and have a splash! The quiet and worried Lenore *lucky Lenore good baby* whispers, Missus A I think I've got a hole in my heart, and she lifts up her t-shirt to point to the dent that is her sternum, the sight of which has kept her awake nights for weeks. Oh! oh goodness me – you *do* have a little hole in your heart – you'll have to eat more, fill it up!

When Baby Joseph emerges from the bathroom damp and red-faced, Missus A chirps, Oh there you go! What have you been up to? and she dabs the sweat on his hanging head with the corner of her apron, makes no mention of the hole in the wall or the plaster crumbs on her immaculate linoleum floor.

When Missus A's sister – *Missus D* – visits, the red rose china comes out and the three of them cower behind the couch (knees pressed into our teeny tiny chests, 小心啊). These Children. So Dirty. I don't know how you have them in your house.

I do
object to travelling in close quarters with a dirty
Chinaman, the dirty Chows... Sir,
I would like to let you know what
sort of a place these Chows live in, the dirty dens

make my blood boil. The Chinese nuisance, and their dirty
habits, the unspeakable, loathsome
Chinese dens, wherever the stinking
pig-tailed
caricature of humanity gets a footing. Any European race
ought to exclude the Chinese.
They simply bring disease
and dirt, their dirty habits. The Chow
is a dirty, degraded wretch.
If you want a dirty, undesirable
man, take a Chinaman. What is the attraction for these dirty
Chinese dens? For the malodorous chinky,
these foul-smelling and dirty Chinese shops. Filthy
Chinese are employed handling the fish! The wretch! The dirty
beast! The horrid beast of a Chinaman! The dirty
Fear
of Chinese/'Asian' invasion
is deeply embedded in the New Zealand psyche.
Chinese
street full of filthy Chinese smoking opium.
(One lady is going to see
the management because a Chinaman
sat next to her.) I travelled in a mule cart driven by a dirty
Chinese. The dirty, stinkin' old Chinky
called me everything he could lay his filthy
tongue to. He say plenty good for dirty Chinaman...

Because his mother is too fat to leave the house, Baby Joseph has spent the afternoon slinging mud-slug-gravel soup over the fence, squishing flies into power sockets, painting the carpet flowers with lipstick, mashing it in good.

At 3.30 p.m. he bursts into the kitchen, superhero towel tucked into the neck of his fair-isle jersey, lands hands on hips.

Let's fly our kites!

His sisters are standing at the sink stuffing their faces with Iced Animals, pink green yellow.

Last Chinese New Year Grandfather sent kites, birds for the granddaughters, dragons for the grandsons.

In the garage they find the birds entangled.

Let's fly the dragon, Joseph.

Orrrrright... but you have to let *me* hold it for a long long long long time cos it's *my kite*.

The wind is strong and Cherry runs up the road (just once!) and the dragon is airborne, swooping and diving high above the lampposts. Lenore and Baby Joseph squeal and clap their hands.

The Macallister boys turn up on their bikes. The big one's riding a brand new Chopper with a banana seat, he spits at Cherry's feet. (the asphalt sizzles)

Whatcha got there ching chong?

[Lenore flees]

Hey! It's a dragon, innit? Where'dja get it ching chong?

(唔關你事. 走開!)

Give it to us! Yeah – gizzit ching chong! Gizzit! They throw down their bikes, wrestle the spool out of Cherry's hands.

[Baby Joseph flees]

Whoa! Look at it go!

Cherry stamps her feet, stomps home, runs into Baby Joseph tearing out into the street, face pre-tantrum red, clutching Ping's meat cleaver.

Joseph! What are you doing?

I'm gonna *get* them!

Give me the knife!

It's *my kite*!

The Macallister boys are on their bikes ready to ride off with the dragon in tow when Big Macallister sees Baby Joseph charging grunting meat cleaver flashing and he stands up on the pedals of his Chopper. Shit Wayne – let it go, let it go!

Wee Macallister's face turns homogenised-milk-white and he freezes.

Let it go Wayne! Let it go!

He drops the spool and Baby Joseph storms after him, lands a clanging dent on his rear mudguard.

Joseph! Joseph! Come back! The kite, the kite!

The wind is strong and the spool is tap-tap-tapping on the asphalt, string unravelling, the dragon soaring so high they can barely make out the flames.

Practitioners of the Oriental
martial arts use a large range of weapons.

(that summer joey's meat cleaver tantrums were so famous
the macallister boys didn't dare ching chong us again)

English Mittens

What strikes one afresh at every
turn is the way in which,
in almost everything, the Chinaman
adheres to the customs of his race. Apparently it never
occurs to him to adopt the customs of the European.

the new baby has her eyes closed, a pale-blue hat on her head, and her hands bound in white mittens so she doesn't scratch her face and cry. in (our) chinese the word for scratch is *wah* 搲 and the word for cry is *hook* 哭 – so if the baby wahs her face she will hook. I look at my sister's face: the folded eyes, the barely nose, flat cheeks glowing like a sixty-watt lightbulb, and that's when it comes to me, that's when I know: that even if we spend the next hundred years carving roast lamb on sundays, buttering white bread, and boiling brussels sprouts, we could never be them, nor they us, because if someone were to *hook* an english baby's face she would *wah!* – even if she had her mittens on.

In the garage she drops the bike, wipes her face on the back of her sleeve. They had jabbed their bony elbows into her ribs hoicked into her basket *Piss off ya Chinese bitch!* gravelled her spokes *Fuck off back to China!* groped her shiny silver bell *ding! ding! ding!* She landed on her hip in the gutter (gagging on their 鬼仔 sweat). They never dared to chant the comeback so popular with Kiwi kids: *sticks and stones may break my bones but names will never hurt me.*

Star Trek's beaming on the TV, coals glowing in the grate (the house cold, as always), Lenore and Baby Joseph on their knees, palms black, opening the day's stack of newspapers on the coffee table, her mother in the kitchen wiping the bench with a tea towel, looking up at her tear-stained-pebble-stung face, buttoning up her work smock, just heat this up for dinner ok?

English boy
veeery cheeky
While the Chinese
were protected under
British law, verbal abuse,
vandalism and physical
assault were commonplace
and perceived by many
to be 'high-spirited
pranks'. *what can*
you do? nothing
can do 冇辦法

The sooner
the old British ideal
of *sport for its own sake*
is recaptured
in the international arena,
the better life will be
for the world-at-large.

Like the Queen, Cherry does not attend the opening ceremony. She is not in the stadium to see Prince Philip inspect the military guard of honour, she is not there to see the raising of the flags, or to hear Steve Allen sing 'Join Together' to rousing applause, she is not one of the 2500 children standing in a square of Ns and Zs in the middle of the athletic track. (When they handed out the slick red, white and blue capes, the teacher, Miss J (whose thick red hair hung like a horse's tail past the hem of her miniskirt) said, Sorry dear, your name is not on The List).

On the day, it really doesn't matter. Like the Queen, Cherry watches the opening ceremony on a Brand New Television Set, surrounded by her family.

She wakes to the television playing Baby Joseph screaming the meat cleaver banging head thumping chest aching throat itching cigarette smoke wafting in from the living room the night pressing cold against the windows 吃飯! chairs scraping china bowls rattling her father booming, Cherry 呢!

Angry footsteps down the hall. Click of the light switch, 100-watt-whiff of fishandchipgrease – blankets off! and there she is (there I was   ) a foetus (a baby   ) (*her* baby   ) shaking knees-to-chest on the sweat-soaked mattress.

吃飯! Not hungry Mama. Why you not listen to me! (   ) 飲湯! Sharp-knuckled imperative across the right temple – You Not Even Sick. (((   ))) 起身!

Soon as the lunch crowd thins he's home (alone!) briny from the morning's snapper/groper/blue cod, he greets her with a shout, You right?

And she nods, smile hidden under the blanket.

Wednesday's gift was a drawing pad and felt tip pens, Friday's a book of splendorous trees too-heavy on her aching chest,

today, a cuckoo clock. He sets it up on the bookshelf next to her collection of cornflake figurines, where she can see it from the bed,

the clock ticks and their eyes shine, and when the cuckoo pops out on the stroke of two – Cuckoo! Cuckoo! Cuckoo! – she shrieks laughs coughs heaves rattles the bedhead he scrambles for water and she gulps, gasps, whimpers,

and in those moments a pearl is seeded in the father, the daughter, the walls of the house.

dear miss j
sorry cherry couldn't go to school.
the doctor said she was very sick
with the new moania.
yours sincere-ly,
~~cherry~~ mrs chin

What did you do in the holidays? Did you go away?

No Miss.

What did you get up to then?

(fried fish, burned my hands on the oil) Did some cooking with my mum.

That sounds like fun. What did you make?

We cooked fish and... sausages... on the barbeque.

Did you get together with your *whole family*? I bet there were lots of people. What else did you eat? Dumplings? Fried rice?

Yeah.

We had a lot of nice hot days, didn't we?

(frying fish without fans in the shop) Yeah.

What else did you get up to?

(opened fifty bundles of newspapers) Lots of reading.

Well! Aren't you good?

The Chinese
are not fond of the sunlight, and most
of the rooms are dark and depressing.
How the children can grow up healthy is one of the secrets
of this strange race. But they grow up in the darkness
and the smell and take their exercise in a tiny
backyard among the rubbish. And
they seem happy enough.

They are at the movies while their mother naps, cocooned in the red faux velvet of the living room, rag-toys lined up on the sofa, potato chips in blue-and-white rice bowls.

Ten minutes into The Flintstones, someone's hand is in someone else's bowl.

Slap. Ow! Stop it! Now look what you've done!

Chips all over the flowery carpet. (eggshells)

Whack. Don't! Shush!

A bowl sails, shatters on the hearth.

Footsteps bruising in the hall,
they all dive for the cushions – shaft of light and their mother-dark marches in wooden coathanger in hand whacks bottoms legs arms heads 殺你! 殺你! 殺你! until they all fall down cowering on the carpet, arms clamped around their cushion-helmet heads.

(the bathtub ringed with a dozen grey
bands)

MOTHER'S DAY GIFT SUGGESTIONS

Sunbeam Mixmaster Mixer

Escort Pop-up Toaster

Ralta Salon Hairdryer

Royal Suite Towels (Boxed Set)

Hoover Spray Steam and Dry Iron

Hay Nest of Tables

Clothes Trolley

Coal Hod

Vanity Chair

When the doctor says, Stan, your wife's blood pressure is dangerously high she needs to be on complete bed-rest, Ping shuffles out to the car in her dressing gown, the peonies on her slippers unravelling.

They move in with AuntyBettyUncleJack& TraceyBrendaKatrina, where life is late afternoons at the library, dandelion chains on the back verandah, book mountains on the beds, Popsicles, Pebbles, bubbles in the clawfoot bath, comics by the fire on too-tired-for-school-days, sucking 話梅 (breathing).

They had all Baby Joseph's clothes washed and ready and a name picked out – Johnson (like the baby powder).

For weeks the new baby remains nameless.

Ping: I like Johnson.
Cherry [eye roll]: Boys' name?
Stan: Joan.
Cherry: Old!
Lenore: Mona.
Cherry: Moaner?
Joseph: Maisie!
Ping: Ugh.
Lenore: Daisy?
Joseph: Rosie?
Cherry: Robin.
Joseph: Batman!
Lenore: Sky?
Joseph: Star! Twinkle Twinkle Little Star ...light.

They name the new baby 'Starlit'. Ping dresses the new baby in Baby Joseph's old clothes. When people tell her what a cute little boy she has, she doesn't bother to correct them. Nor does she intervene when Baby Joseph clocks the new baby on the head with his string of wooden ducks.

I am First
Wife Number
Four Daughter
Number Four
Sister I got three
children first-born
is the girl second-
born 'nother girl
Number One is
the Boy

In the 1970s,
New Zealand began to break
away from Great Britain to develop a new identity.
We began to see
ourselves as part of Asia
and the Pacific rather
than some far-flung British outpost, and the Māori
people and their language and culture were gifted with
greater recognition at this time.

Social Studies:

1908–1952: Naturalisation of Chinese ceased.

1917–1977: Registration of Aliens Act. All Chinese (neither born nor naturalised in New Zealand) required to register.

Mister C: What two cultures do we have in New Zealand?

Cherry: Um... the Māori and the Pākehā?

Mister C: What do you think of that?

Cherry doesn't know what The Sounds are, but looking at the waves in Missus C's hair, she reckons it must be someplace 'high-class' (as her mother would say), with white sand, crystal-blue water and long-anchored yachts with names like Serenity, Felicity, Penelope.

Would you like to feed our pussycat while we're away darling? We have an arrangement with the butcher, all you have to do is pick up the meat, we'll leave the hose dripping in the bowl. Missus C is crouching beneath the pōhutakawa tree tsk-tsk-tsk-ing at the fat grey loaf rising from the leaves.

She's quite happy outside, aren't you Agatha? She rubs Agatha's head, stands and unfurls a stringy blond arm toward the hedge like a showgirl introducing a late-model car.

You can use the swimming pool on hot days if you like, she purrs, smiling broadly, and Cherry notices that her top incisors overlap like fingers crossed for luck.

(the mission.) each day it began with the morning poo, baba's coffee steaming kitchen tiles greased with the splatter of wok-fried food, starlit dribbling marmite in the highchair, burning toast smoking the kitchen sepia. baba would hand out the cadbury's after we'd tied our tattered shoes and slid into the backseat of the rusty fusty vauxhall viva. by the time we got to school our eyes were wide as walnuts. stay out of the sun, our mother would warn, *too-dark-like-a-māori.* but I knew I had to be brown – it was the colour of everyone-and-everything-in-the-world-that-wasn't-white. The sounds of Cantonese were so ridiculed they refused to speak it outside the home, but speaking Māori was 'cool' – they all learned to kia ora, complain about their whanau(s), poke fun at their fathers' puku(s).

Stan launches SkyrocketsCatherineWheelsMtVesuvius from empty milk bottles. (in celebration of the failure of the gunpowder plot in england more than 300 years ago) They all twirl sparklers on the front steps in their wonky-hemmed skirts and shorts, knees scabby, faces grey and pinched like the dusk.

Ping is washing up in the kitchen when a man thrusts his face into the open window above the sink. She jumps at the sight of his bushy black eyebrows arched above the sill. 哎呀 *burglar!*

Good night for it, ay?

burglar been drinking the beer. She gropes for the bread knife beneath the suds.

You got any Leeds? or Fanta? For the kids? It's me... Rick.

Ohhh... you are Rae-the-husband... No... sorry.

Have a good night, he sways and bows and she pulls the window shut shaking.

In the morning the inside of their letterbox is burnt black (bet it was the macallisters), the driveway littered with spent rockets, Tom Thumbs, Double Happies.

that summer was blue skies sprinklers pink *icy-cream* sandwiches, mama singing *call me when the* 肥婆 *come I need butter make the pike-a-lit*, joey smashing wooden ducks through the frosted front door, on my knees on the concrete pasting the hole (where the world gets in) with the classifieds: houses to let – cars for sale – situations vacant – lenore waving bloody underwear beneath the noses of our nice white friends, mama pale and bilious thump-thump-thumping baba's shirts on the washboard ribbed like a condom: you dead man you dead man I hate you the most, you dead man you dead man I hate you the most.

For the Good Husband

for the good husband
must be have
good figure 有前有後
show off little bit you
know and wear
the make-up girl
have to be look pretty
otherway the man
can't see you

Cherry can't get over the change in Delia, her power-socket hair bleached blonde, black-kohl eyes, brown-skin breasts, the lip gloss, the bright yellow Afro comb, skirt so short the frayed edges of her knickers hang below the hem, shirt so threadbare Dan and Solly sitting behind them wrestle to ping her emphatically black bra straps. (the new delia is dazzling, unravelling)

The year's first earthquake drill, crouched beneath their desks, Delia's haunches dishevelling her grey-white knee-socks, Juicy Fruit breath. What'dja do in the holidays? ( ) Wanna know what I did? You know what fuck means? say it, go on say it... fuck. f u c k. fuuuuck.

Cherry has a crush two doors down. Shane has hair like Leif Garrett, wears sunglasses inside, rides a Red Honda Motorbike. 250cc.

Cruising Baby Joseph's skateboard in her exotically embroidered Hong Kong flares (insides fizzing like yeast) she sails down the hill past his house 哎呀! *danger very danger!* flips on a rock lands on the asphalt (skin my tailbone).

When the rat, mouth agape and monstrously fat, lands with a thud on the dissection mat, Cherry and Delia spit out their gum, wedge it beneath the rim of the lab table, roll up their sleeves. Delia picks up the scalpel.

Here, you wanna be a nurse don't you?

People, not rats.

Get used to blood and guts Cherrio.

Cherrio pokes the rat with the scalpel, flips it onto its back.

Now what?

I'll hold the arms.

She stabs the blade just below the rat's ribcage, scores a line down the middle of its swollen belly,

Forceps and scissors?

peels back the damp fur, cuts into the abdominal wall. The rat's legs are splayed and its tiny feet move up and down as she snips.

(forgive me)

What'd you say?

Nothin'.

Whoa... what are all these red balls?

Babies, by the look of it.

Mister H, the optometrist: Your daughter needs to wear her glasses all the time.

Ping: Nooooo – she OK.

Mister H: Mrs Chin. She can't read the biggest letters on the chart without them.

Ping: 哎呀… 爸爸 doesn't like. Uncle Jack doesn't like. Look terrible!

Cherry: But –

Ping: *Very hard to get the boyfriend.*

Cherry: But –

Ping: You see the *bride* wearing the glasses?

Cherry: But –

Ping: Never see such thing!

Cherry: I can't see without them –

Ping: Then better not see.

Delia can hear dead people talk. After school at the local cemetery, she and Cherry sit between the graves recording voices with a tape deck, a Ouija board and Delia's father's whisky glass spelling messages from the spirit world. Delia has thick dark lashes, when she channels they twitch like spiders wrestling out of her eye sockets.

When night falls they turn on the radio, shake out their hair between the headstones – they're Cathy-and-Heathcliff zombies out in the frosty ghost-y air so cold (so fucking cold).

In the 5.30 p.m. dark Cherry stands tiptoe on the bedroom sill, hangs out the window clutching Stan's binoculars. Shane is in the garage two doors down tinkering on his Honda, revving up the engine... (leaning into the wind... his shoulder fierce beneath my cheek...)

Shaft of light – Lenore – the door!

What are you doing?

Shhhhhh...

looking at the stars

Evening smells like coal, slammed dishes. Lenore's at the table, face in a bowl, pinching her nose with a blood-soaked flannel. Enter Ping, clapping her hands. Why You Still Bleeding!

Delia says the curse is karma. Cherry is bedridden three days a month and she wonders if it's got anything to do with the skateboard accident 哎呀 *danger, very danger*. Really, Delia tsks, you should use tampons much less mess easier later for you know when you finally wash your hair and get a boyfriend. They are sealed behind the glass doors in Delia's living room with the family cats Mungo and Mucky, all of them inhaling Delia's mother's chain of hand-rolled cigarettes. That afternoon between English and Biology a large blot appeared on the back of Cherry's skirt, she swung it to the left, tied her jersey round her waist and shuffled from class to class to minimise the flow before Delia (dear delia) offered a luxurious Barbie-doll-mattress-sized pad wrapped in the morning's front page news.

you know Jennifer? Aunty
Pat sister-in-law the daughter
The Chinese New Zealand
woman is produced
from 'differential
family relations' ***she***
big tummy! you know
why? she go camping
with the boy, danger
very danger 哎呀
sixteen mother 爛女!

As Jennifer's tummy grows bigger and rounder so do her eyes – like Violet Beauregarde she can hardly believe what's happening to her body – then, when it looks like she couldn't possibly get any bigger, she disappears – all of a sudden – like a popped balloon.

Did Jennifer have the baby?
Who?
Jennifer. Haven't seen her for a long time.
Her mother kick out.
No way. Where'd she go?
She dead girl. 死女.

The most extraordinary
thing about the Chinese woman
is that she curls
her hair and
dances.

You come. Meet more Chinese friend.
Who's getting married this time?
You know Jello?
Who?
Jello, Barba the big brother.
You mean *Gerald*? *Barbara's* brother?
Jello mother 介紹 *very nice girl.*
China girl?
Beautiful... white skin.
Ugh.
靚女!
No one here good enough for him?
Here Chinese girl too fussy! Jello veeery good boy, always listen mother father *never argue,* he got the good job, nearly doctor!
He's a dentist, Ma.
Den-tit better! No sick people, don't have to talk, more money, Jello wife lucky girl, Jello 真係 veeery good husband.

The Assembly Hall, where the reception
for over 600 guests was held, presented an exotic
and colourful spectacle
created by the many Chinese
women who wore richly embroidered
but simple Chinese dress They did their best
to confine their Chineseness to their fruit
shops, market gardens, and double-happy weddings
offset
by the conventional attire of the many European
guests.

Saturday night 囍 at the Wintergarden. Cherry and Ping stepping into the foyer. Oh my god *love* that dress! (oh my god, it's barbara) I made one exactly the same last year except *mine* is *real silk* – Vogue two-zero-four-two? Cherry very good sewing, I teaching her – Ping puffs out her heavily sequinned chest, breasts ablaze – You look very nice, Barba. Barba grins wide, checks the seating plan, Cherry keeps her teeth to herself. Ping pinches the flesh in her daughter's upper arm [sotto voce]: 哎呀 you little bit fat now. (and you have a face like a 叉燒包)

They follow Barbara, Cherry stomping, past all the girls in their frizzy perms and homemade silk-taffeta-polyester dresses, the boys stiff and shiny with VO5. Here we are, says Barbara. They are seated opposite Rex and his mum at the back of the (~~poultry farm~~) banquet hall. Rex pulls at the skinny leather tie around his blue-starched no-neck, raises his eyebrows, the mothers screech and squawk. 好耐冇見! 你最近點啊? 忙唔忙啊? What's JockKenPatsyMary up to? MichelleLisaBrandonDaniel? What they study now? (How to Be a Doctor / Dentist / Accountant / Wife). Got the boyfriend girlfriend yet? 哎呀快啲介紹! Shhhhhhhh! Shhhhhhhh! Ding ding ding!

Good evening ladies and gentlemen, let's talk about Gerald... first pub crawl... chucked up in the Star Fountain... and at the Remarkables... beef and cheese pie all over the windscreen... rolled the old man's Kingswood into the Waimak... wild... hypothermia... how pretty the bridesmaids look (in salmon pink) tonight... and the bride so beautiful (So Dutiful)... how lucky is Gerald (how lucky his parents) how lucky 佢媽介紹... ding ding ding!

Let us propose a toast to Connie and Gilbert. Congratulations on the wedding of another son, you must be so proud! Let's celebrate your children... your achievements... success! (dying...) God bless! (...for a screwdriver) They have all inherited Connie's good looks [Laughter] ... so respectful and obedient! Let's stand now and sing [Barbara playing the piano] *We will never grow old...* Soberly they raise their glasses (asti riccadonna / sparkling water / tepid orange juice) to Connie and Gilbert, Fine Raisers of Obedient Offspring.

They have not been out further than the shops at the end of the street on the back of his Honda 250cc. He did invite her swimming in their Para Pool once, just the two of them it would've been, but her mother forbade it, *Nooooo,* she said, *stay inside tan too dark,* pinch-bruising her arm and dragging her off to a(nother) pink carnation Chinese wedding, where she danced all night with a fumbling Pākehā boy, who tore her brand new 'silken' pantyhose in the coatroom (that smelled of opium and ajax) while the band played the chicken dance. Prompted by the interviewer, she stated that even if her parents did not approve she would certainly consider marriage to a Pākehā man if she were in love with him.

What is the point of this anecdote? Is this a story
about assimilation
or – god forbid – miscegenation? This
Cherry character
doesn't seem very... Chinese.
Could you put her in a *chong-sam*
or have her wipe a few grains of rice
from her mouth... or explore the Pākehā boy's point of view
perhaps? How does he feel kissing this exotic
Chinese girl? Does she taste like
soy sauce?

(I have never worn a *cheongsam*)

(he tasted like cheddar cheese)

Sunday Gardening

the god
he everywhere
he see all the thing
you put the broom up
make the god
angry then hard
life

It's ten-thirty at night and there's a low rumble in the kitchen.

Grandfather is dead.

The brothers sit late, smoking cigarettes and drinking tea.

Not a word is spoken on the flight over.

They bury Grandfather in a cemetery on the side of a hill overlooking the city, steep graves packed in tiered rows: an amphitheatre of headstones looking down on the city below.

They take it in turns to pay their last respects, bowing three times deeply, quickly. Stan trips and the incense stick flies out of his hand, lands in a vase of plastic flowers on the terrace below. [Grandmother hmmphs].

The headstone is engraved in gold and inlaid with a black-and-white photograph of Grandfather in his prime, skin smooth and cheeks fat and prosperous. Great-Grandfather would've been proud.

With Stan away, Ping has Rick helping out in the shop. She likes him because he's half-Chinese and only once flicked cigarette ash into the fish batter. Now and then he *smell like the beer* but he's happy to take on Stan's work, going early to the market, filleting fish, chatting to customers while she cooks.

It's all going well until the night Ping gets a call from Dawn behind the dairy.

Stan home?

No – she – he – go to Hong Kong.

You know your shop's on fire? Fire truck's there now.

There are puddles on the cement floor. Flame-licked walls. Blackened ceiling. Stack of newspaper ash. The greasy towel Rick had flung over the two-bar heater.

Starlit stands stripped to the waist.

Doctor B has declared 'bronchitis', he's scrawling a solution. So, he says, without looking up, how are you, Mrs Chin?

Tired... and, Ping leans forward, hand at her throat, Sometime my heart go *boom-boom-boom...*

How many hours are you working?

Ah... Stan go to Hong Kong, I go to work seven clock, come home eight clock.

When's Stan coming back?

Two week.

How many days will you work then – when he comes back?

Sunday day off, afternoon clean the shop.

Seven days! With four children? (we work too)

Starlit is getting goosebumps, she rubs her upper arms, eyes the balled-up skivvy in Ping's wringing hands.

Have to.

Mrs Chin – Doctor B peers over his glasses like a courtroom judge – Keep working like this and you'll be *dead before you're fifty.* (her heart??)

No choice – English no good.

You can *learn* English, go to school.

Before I go – but now no time.

Then try reading the newspaper every day.

'Sunday Gardening. Chinese Fined.'
Evening Post. 10 Mar 1914.
Dunedin.
At the Police Court this morning a Chinese
market gardener was fined
5s and costs for working
at his calling on Sunday.

'Working on Sunday.'
Ashburton Guardian. 23 April 1908.
Christchurch.
A Chinese
market gardener was today fined
10s, and two Chinese employees 5s each,
for carrying on their work,
at Marshlands, on Sunday,
within view from a public street.

'Sunday Work.'
Taranaki Daily News. 3 Aug 1907.
Wellington.
Three Chinese
gardeners at Otaki were fined
1s each and costs for working on Sunday,
and warned they would be severely
dealt with if they offended again.

1898:
Old Age Pensions Act. Chinese and other 'Asiatics',
including those who have been naturalised, ineligible.

Happy Valley.

Grandmother is sitting by the window staring at the racecourse below. [Rumble of machines, falling mortar down the hill.] She wedges a cushion behind her back, folds her arms across her chest.

Around Ping's kitchen table

the daughters-in-law fuss: She'll be cold...
they worry: She won't understand a word...
and they fight: She's *not* staying with *me.*

The day Cherry takes a cup of chopped cheese to school she discovers her latest crush is sleeping with the class mouse. I saw them, says Delia, delighting in her audience, *buying condoms from the chemist*. The girls all scoff. No way! Not her!

In Mister P's English class they watch the lovers ignore one another, she beneath her greasy fringe, he behind his boarish demeanour, carefully cultivated to conceal all signs of tenderness.

Mister P, today in lime-green pants suit & platform boots, notes their inattention. Are you listening to me girls?

Cherry: Nope!

Mister P (drama queen) points a finger at the door.

Which is how Cherry finds herself in the park, napping on the creek bank long enough to be late to cooking class and waking with a start – oh my god, the cheese!

In the home ec kitchen, Cherry hides the late-night-cubed Cheddar sealed in a plastic cup with lunch paper and a greasy rubber band. Everyone Else has brought their cheese in neat stay-at-home-mum Tupperware tubs with plastic lids that click on closing. Everyone Else's cheese is light and delicate and fluffy (because it has been grated). Cherry's cheese is an ugly meat-cleavered mess and she hurries to fold it into the bowl of flour and milk – but Delia is watching.

That's too much butter.

No, it's not.

After scones, her mother's at the school gate in the Fiat, early and anxious, her siblings slouched in the back seat, the engine running. When she slams the door, steam shoots from the bonnet with a hiss and she screams: It's gonna blow up! Her brother shouts: Quick! Get out! It's gonna blow up! They all leap out and run across the street leaving their mother clutching the steering wheel, face white as her work smock.

no time to eat
even one bowl
the rice no time
真係冇時間
even 屙屎

What is that smell?

Tiger balm, she puts it on every night.

What's with all the newspapers? Do you have to clean in there?

Ugh. Plastic bags everywhere – and baby powder.

Shhh! She's right there.

Don't worry, all she knows is 'hello bye-bye *good boy*'.

She's eighty... something – how much Chinese do you know?

一句唔識講.

Four words.

Five.

After school she finds her father sprawled flat on his back in the bedroom, face glowing from the four o'clock sun filtered through red faux velvet, an almost-empty bottle of cough mixture sticky on the bedside table.

Ba?

Stan turns his head. Give me medicine.

How much have you had? She wipes the bottle with his handkerchief, he sucks down what's left of the syrup.

At the shop Ping's shuffling baskets in the bubbling vats. Rick's taking orders, sprinkling salt and wrapping.

Where's Stan? Got the night off? It's Mister R, the ruddy-cheeked principal of the local primary school.

Rick says, Having a rest at home, bit tired.

Ping tilts a basket, lets the oil drain.

Leaving the wife to do all the work, eh?

Splotch of hot oil lands on the back of the wife's hand, she wipes it on the front of her smock, licks it.

Although she is waiting in the hall, Cherry is startled by Doctor B's large grey frame and the rap-rap-rap of his fat-knuckled fist on the frosted glass. She opens the door and, overcome by the smell of chimney smoke and mothballs and the doctor's imperious boom ('Where's your father!') – flattens herself against the wall to let him pass.

Flu, Stan?

Feel terrible, Doctor B, terrible.

The doctor roams his stethoscope across Stan's chest, scratches on a pad, slaps a prescription on the sticky ring left by the syrup bottle.

Doubling the dose, Stan finishes the antibiotics in three days. When he gets up in the night to go to the toilet, the room tips and he claws at the swaying walls. Ping pulls the blankets up to her nose, eyes wide at the sight of her husband's shadow flailing around the room like some pre-phosphorescent fire.

In the vermilion darkness of the bedroom, Doctor Gin, a family friend, pumps the sphygmomanometer and as the cuff deflates he squints at the falling mercury, 哎呀哎呀哎呀.

人人 *say*
is my fault
she say I must
be upset him
too much make
the high blood
pressure my fault

Stan likes the hospital food, especially the stewed apples and corned beef.

The damage occurred in the cerebellum, the resident doctor tells Ping, who nods her head and says, I see. That's why he's having problems with his balance. He can work? We'll... monitor his progress.

Stan's favourite seat is on the front porch, the arms of the chair flat and wide, good for coffee cups, bowls and books, the lull of passing traffic good for sleep.

Afternoons he wakes to crunching gravel and Cherry: face red, shirt-tails loose, satchel hanging off the back of her bike.

When he staggers to the toilet, legs wide, she places a steaming bowl of pork mince 粥 (of course, two hands) on the arm of his chair. Hey! he shouts, where's the soy sauce?

They sell *Bob's Fish Supply* to Rick.

Ping and Lenore get work in a factory that makes cheap wool-blend coats. In the tearoom – small, dark and windowless, the other workers huddle and smoke and the roof leaks when it rains.

Cherry works weekends at the local hospital where rich people have their tonsils, cataracts and abdominal fat removed, the casual staff's change room is a broom cupboard and the nights, black tea & Huntley Palmer cream crackers (and snoozing in the armchair when sister lois is away   ).

Compared to frying fish the work is easy.

Steam the coats! Brush off the fluff!

Could I trouble you for a glass of water dear? Would you mind straightening the sheets?

Five a.m.: Roll the butterballs for breakfast – 1.5cm wide, three per tray.

Four p.m.: Wheel the racks to the back – black with black, beige with beige (rage rage!   ) – line 'em up *straight* for goodness sake!

The doctor tells them Grandmother has liver failure, her eyes are yellow and her blood is full of bile.

Ping: She very angry something.
Maisie: She not happy here.
Betty: She not understand.
(I don't understand)

After they take out her gall bladder, Grandmother dies
in the hospital. Stan and Robert choose the gravestone: black granite with their mother's origins engraved in gold. The service is held in the paths of righteousness at St Augustine's Anglican Church. They hum English hymns and mouth English prayers.
(一句唔識講)

The Reverend Mister
Don: With regard to the question of the admission
of Chinese women,
it is very hard
to know just what to do.

It is a cool eight-degree day, the second sunniest August since records began in 1949. Despite the midday glare and the sombreness of the occasion, not one of them is wearing sunglasses. They leave Grandmother to rest beneath a eucalyptus tree, 5988 miles from Lee May-Yun born San Ning County, Canton Province. To the left of her, Edgar Thornton, dearly beloved husband of Olive, to the right of her, Walter Sharp, Gone Fishing.

Translations

The Chinese phrases in *Chinese Fish* are hybrid Cantonese-Taishanese (Hoisan-wa), which reflects the author's lived experience with these languages. (Words and phrases that do not appear here are translated within the poems.)

新寧	San Ning – county in (old) Canton province, China; pre-1914 name for Taishan / Hoisan county, Guangdong, China
臺山	Taishan / Hoisan – county in Guangdong, China
菊花茶	chrysanthemum tea
增城	Jung Seng – county in Guangdong, China
冰室	Hong Kong style café; literally, 'ice house'
叉燒包	BBQ pork bun
'香片茶'	'Jasmine Tea'

Happy Valley

'In the summer of 1963'

算命先生	fortune teller
靚仔	handsome young man
新金山	New Gold Mountain

'When the mother runs out of push'

好好	very good

'soon as you born'

人人	Grandmother (paternal, Taishanese)
粥	rice porridge / congee

'There are two weeks in the hospital'

豬腳薑醋	pig's feet, ginger and vinegar soup

'人人 see'

人人	Grandmother (paternal, Taishanese)

'then I taking you home'

爺爺	Grandfather (paternal)
人人	Grandmother (paternal, Taishanese)

'The 滿月 party'

滿月	celebration for babies at one month of age
龍	Dragon
長衫	cheongsam
普洱	Pu'er, tea traditionally grown in Yunnan

'I so tire my dress'

哎呀	oh my god
爸爸	Baba / Father / Dad

'It's August, sticky'

爸爸	Baba / Father / Dad
做乜啊	What's up? / What are you doing?
阿爺	Grandfather (paternal)
大家姐	eldest sister

'The father puts on his best tie'

叉燒包	BBQ pork buns
阿爺	Grandfather (paternal)

Paradise

'every day I stay'

西餐	Western food

'I in the bath'

哎呀	oh my god
唔好哭唔好哭唔好哭	don't cry don't cry don't cry

Good Luck and Plenty

'why you talk'

鬼佬鬼婆	colloquial term for Pākehā men and women

'In the classroom'

一句唔識講	can't even speak one word / sentence
媽媽！媽媽?	Mama! Mama?

'In the eyes of the mainstream'

糉	sticky rice parcel
臘腸	Chinese sausage

'哎呀! What's the matter with Cherry?'

哎呀!	Oh my god!
冬菇	shiitake mushrooms
阿爺	Grandfather (paternal)

'lunch is roast chicken'

阿爺	Grandfather (paternal)

'when 爺爺 stay'

爺爺	Grandfather (paternal)

'It's twenty-four degrees'

你咁乖仔嘅!	You're such a good boy!
多謝爺爺多謝	Thank you Grandfather thank you

'you was seven'

爸爸	Baba / Dad / father

Chinese Fish

'after school they watch Johnny'

爸爸	Baba / Dad / father

'shop VERY clean'

死鬼佬	dead / damn Pākehā man
哎呀	oh my god
死鬼佬最憎...	dead / damn Pākehā man, most hateful...

'When Ping discovers'

哎呀 哎呀 哎呀 四四四... 死死死	oh my god oh my god oh my god, four four four... dead dead dead / damn damn damn

'Missus A lives in a tiny'

小心啊	(have a) small heart / be careful

'Because his mother is too fat'

唔關你事. 走開!	None of your business, go away!

English Mittens

'In the garage'

鬼仔	colloquial term for Pākehā boy

'She wakes to the television'

吃飯!	Time to eat!
呢!	What about [Cherry]?
飲湯!	Drink / have (some) soup!
起身!	Get up!

'They are at the movies'

殺你! 殺你! 殺你! [I'll] kill you! kill you! kill you!

'When the doctor says'

話梅 dried plum(s)

'Stan launches Skyrockets'

哎呀 oh my god

'that summer was blue skies'

肥婆 fat woman

For the Good Husband

'Cherry has a crush'

哎呀! oh my god!

'Mister H, the optometrist'

哎呀... 爸爸 Oh my god... Baba / Dad

'Delia says the curse'

哎呀 oh my god

'you know Jennifer?'

哎呀	oh my god
爛女!	broken / bad girl!

'did Jennifer have the baby?'

死女 dead / damn girl

'You come. Meet more Chinese'

介紹	introduce
靚女!	beautiful girl!
真係	really is

'Saturday night 囍 at the Wintergarden.'

囍 double happiness / double happy

哎呀　　Oh my god
叉燒包　　BBQ pork bun
好耐冇見! 你最近點啊? 忙唔忙啊?　　Long time no see! How have you been? Been busy?
哎呀 – 快啲介紹!　　Oh my god – hurry up and set them up! (with someone)
佢媽介紹　　His mother introduced them (to each other)

Sunday Gardening

'no time to eat'
真係冇時間　　really don't have time
屙屎　　(to) take a shit

'What is that smell?'
一句唔識講　　can't even speak one word / sentence

'Doubling the dose'
哎呀哎呀哎呀　　oh my god oh my god oh my god

'人人 say is'
人人　　Grandmother (paternal, Taishanese)

'Stan likes the hospital food'
粥　　rice porridge / congee

'After they take out her gall bladder'
一句唔識講　　can't even speak one word / sentence

Notes

Chinese Fish has been adapted from 'Sunday Gardening: The Adventures of John Chinaman on the New Gold Mountain', the creative component of the author's PhD thesis, *Beneath the Long White Cloud: Settler Chinese Women's Storytelling in Aotearoa New* Zealand, completed at the University of Melbourne, 2016. Phrases and sentences from the critical component of the thesis, including references to legislation from Nigel Murphy, *Guide to Laws and Policies Relating to the Chinese in New Zealand 1871–1997*, New Zealand Chinese Association (2008), are included in grey text.

Illustrations by Zachary RM Wong.

Happy Valley

'Due to the lack' includes phrases – in parentheses – borrowed and adapted from 'Celestial Satyrs, How Chow Molls Are Made'. *NZ Truth*. 9 Nov 1907: 5.

Paradise

'LOVINGLY' is inspired by an advertisement for Formica Furniture. Mair & Co. *The Press*. 3 May 1956: 18.

'Chinese women look charming' includes phrases borrowed and adapted from 'No Paris Fashions.' *Opunake Times*. 12 July 1927: 4; 'Factories in China.' *New Zealand Herald*. 26 Nov 1925: 7.

Good Luck and Plenty

'Please. If we must have immigrants' includes phrases borrowed and adapted from Letter to the Editor. *Press*. 9 Oct 1964: 14.

'Mighty Saving!' is inspired by Tiger Tea. Four Square New World. Advertisement. *The Press*. 27 October 1971: 10.

'Angie's living room' includes an allusion to Neil Diamond's 'Song Sung Blue.' Uni, 1972.

'Lunch is roast chicken' includes an allusion to Carly Simon's 'You're So Vain.' Elektra, 1972.

'The Chinese woman' includes phrases borrowed from 'Chinese Cosmetics.' *Poverty Bay Herald*. 6 Feb 1937: 10.

'you was seven' includes a reference to Rey Chow, 'Virtuous Transactions: A Reading of Three Stories by Ling Shuhua.' *Gender Politics in Modern China: Writing and Feminism*. Ed. Tani E. Barlow. Durham: Duke University Press, 1993: 94–96.

Chinese Fish

'Chinese food' is borrowed and adapted from 'Chinatown in Wellington. Something about "John's" Home Life.' *Evening Post*. 24 Dec 1904: 5.

'The rules laid down' is borrowed and adapted from 'The Whole Duty of Woman from a Chinese Point of View.' *Bruce Herald*. 10 Oct 1876: 7.

'Just going to have a look round' is borrowed and adapted from 'Chinatown in Wellington. Something About "John's" Home Life.' *Evening Post*. 24 Dec 1904: 5.

'FRACAS' is borrowed and adapted from 'Fracas in a Laundry: European v Chinese.' *Evening Post*. 2 May 1910: 7.

'I do' includes excerpts borrowed and adapted from: 'Chinese Customs.' *Oamaru Mail*. 14 Aug 1894: 3; 'The Chow Curse.' *NZ Truth*. 9 Nov 1907: 6; 'Public Nuisances.' *Western Star*. 24 Apr 1880: 5; 'Chinese Concubines.' *NZ Truth*. 1 Feb 1908: 5; 'Chinese Fruiterers.' *Star* (Christchurch). 17 May 1926: 8; 'Still They Come!' *NZ Truth*. 26 Oct 1907: 4; 'Councillors and Chinese.' *Evening Star*. 12 Jun 1913: 2; 'The Fretful Porcupine.' *Observer*. 15 Sept 1894: 7; 'Death in the Tin.' *North Otago Times*. 4 Jun 1897: 1; 'Novel Bush Cookery.' *Grey River Argus*. 22 Jul 1869: 4; 'Current Topics.' *Lyttelton Times*. 14 Sept 1911: 6; 'The Passing Show.' *Auckland Star*. 14 May 1934: 6; 'Four Cities in One.' *Star* (Christchurch). 17 Nov 1894: 6; 'The Mother of the Child.' *Star* (Christchurch). 2 Dec 1901: 3; 'A Novel Assault Case.' *Wanganui Herald*. 14 Aug 1890: 3.

English Mittens

'What strikes one afresh' is borrowed and adapted from 'Chinatown in Wellington. Something about "John's" Home Life.' *Evening Post*. 24 Dec 1904: 5.

'The sooner the old British ideal' is borrowed and adapted from 'British Ideal.' *Gisborne Times*. 2 Jan 1934: 2.

'The Chinese are not fond' is borrowed and adapted from 'Chinatown in Wellington. Something about "John's" Home Life.' *Evening Post*. 24 Dec 1904: 5.

'Mother's Day Gift' items are sourced from 'Christmas Gift Suggestions.' Smiths City Market. Advertisement. *The Press*. 21 Dec 1974: 15.

For the Good Husband

'Delia can hear dead people' includes an allusion to Kate Bush's 'Wuthering Heights.' *The Kick Inside*. EMI Records. 1978.

'you know Jennifer?' includes the phrase 'differential family relations' from Tani E Barlow, 'Theorizing Woman: Funu, Guojia, Jiating (Chinese Woman, Chinese State, Chinese Family).' *Body, Subject and Power in China*. Ed. Angela Zito and Tani E Barlow. Chicago: University of Chicago Press, 1994: 256.

'as Jennifer's tummy grows' includes a reference to Violet Beauregarde from Roald Dahl's *Charlie and the Chocolate Factory*. Alfred A. Knopf, 1964.

'The most extraordinary thing' is borrowed and adapted from 'The Chinese Woman.' *Poverty Bay Herald*. 20 Oct 1934: 10.

'The Assembly Hall' includes a sentence borrowed and adapted from 'Chinese Wedding at Hastings.' *Upper Hutt Leader*. 9 Feb 1956: 7.

'Saturday night 囍 at the Wintergarden' includes a reference to the song 'You Will Never Grow Old', written by Ruth Rand, 1951, and popularised by Nat King Cole and the Nelson Riddle Orchestra. Capitol Records, 1952.

'they have not been out' includes a reference to an interview with 'Jenny' (last name unknown) in 'The Chinese Community', a documentary narrated by Geoff Walker. *Gallery*. NZBC. 25 May 1972.

Sunday Gardening

'Sunday Gardening. Chinese Fined' includes adaptations of extracts from: 'Sunday Gardening. Chinese Fined.' *Evening Post*. 10 Mar 1914: 8; 'Working on Sunday.' *Ashburton Guardian*. 23 April 1908: 4; 'Sunday Work.' *Taranaki Daily News*. 3 Aug 1907: 2.

'The Reverend Mister Don' is borrowed and adapted from 'The Wifeless Chinese.' *Evening Post*. 28 Feb 1905: 5.

Acknowledgements

Thank you to the editors of *The Shanghai Literary Review, Meanjin, Mascara Literary Review, Rabbit, New England Review, Eureka Street, Southerly* and *Poetry New Zealand Yearbook* for publishing earlier versions of some of these poems. *Chinese Fish* began as part of a Creative Writing and Cultural Studies PhD thesis at the University of Melbourne. Thank you to my supervisors Marion May Campbell and Fran Martin, for their generosity and intellectual rigor. I would like to acknowledge the support of a Melbourne Research Scholarship during my doctoral candidature, and the Peter Steele Poetry Award, which enabled an unfettered period of time to work on the manuscript. Heartfelt thanks to: Lisa Gorton, and Aleesha Paz, for their editorial expertise; historical linguist and translator Ely Finch for expert advice on the Cantonese language (I take full responsibility for the final hybrid Cantonese-Taishanese phrases); Zachary RM Wong for the wonderful illustrations; Alison Wong, Coral Campbell and especially Helen Gildfind, for reading multiple versions of the manuscript; and my Chinese-New Zealand-Australian family, for all the memories, near and far.

About the author

Grace Yee lives in Melbourne, on Wurundjeri land. Her poetry has been widely published and anthologised across Australia and internationally, and has been awarded the Patricia Hackett Prize, the Peter Steele Poetry Award, a Creative Fellowship at the State Library Victoria, and grants from Creative Victoria and the Australia Council for the Arts. Grace has taught in the Writing and Literature Program at Deakin University, and in the Creative Writing Program at the University of Melbourne, where she completed a PhD on settler Chinese women's storytelling in Aotearoa New Zealand. graceyeepoet.com